grow up!

D0552220

250 543 138

grow up!

The **101 essential things** every child
needs to know before leaving home

Clare Paterson

RODALE

This edition first published in the UK in 2006 by
Rodale International Ltd
7–10 Chandos Street
London W1G 9AD
www.rodalebooks.co.uk

Copyright © Rodale International Ltd
Text © 2006 Clare Paterson
Illustrations © Jacky Fleming

The moral right of Clare Paterson to be identified as the author of this work has
been asserted in accordance with the Copyright, Designs and Patents Act of 1988.

"To a Daughter Leaving Home" is reprinted from *Poems For My Daughter* by
Linda Pastan, published by Ideals Publications, by permission of the author.

Book design by Paul Ashby

All rights reserved. No part of this publication may be reproduced or transmitted
in any form or by any means, electronic or mechanical, including photocopying,
recording or any other information storage and retrieval system, without the
written permission of the publisher.

Printed and bound in the UK by CPI Bath using acid-free paper from sustainable
sources.

1 3 5 7 9 8 6 4 2

A CIP record for this book is available from the British Library

ISBN-10: 1-4050-9334-X
ISBN-13: 978-1-4050-9334-7

This paperback edition distributed to the book trade by Pan Macmillan Ltd

Notice
The advice in this book is intended as a guide only. It may not be suitable in all
situations or for all individuals. It is not intended as a substitute for professional
medical, legal or other advice. Neither the author nor publisher shall be liable for
any loss or injury arising as a result of information in this book.

Mention of specific companies, organisations or authorities in this book does
not imply endorsement by the publisher, nor does mention of specific companies,
organisations or authorities in the book imply that they endorse the book.

Websites and telephone numbers given in this book were accurate at the time
the book went to press.

RODALE
LIVE YOUR WHOLE LIFE™

We inspire and enable people to improve their lives and the world around them

For my mum,
Beryl Paterson

KIRKLEES CULTURAL AND LEISURE SERVICES	
25O 543 138	
Askews	19-Feb-2007
649.125	£8.99
Ho	CUL42975

Acknowledgements

My grateful thanks are due to all the contributors who kindly offered to share their experiences. Special thanks too to Delia Perry, David Costain, Richard Bull, Robert Heathcote, Daniel Taegtmeyer, Stephen Tall, Sarah Cahn, Richard Merz and Rebecca Paterson for their expertise; to Jenni Trent-Hughes for getting me started; to Jacqueline Burns, Liz Coghill and Carol Franklin for their wisdom and encouragement, and to Jacky Fleming for the wonderful cartoons. To my husband John and my mother Beryl for their unwavering love and support; and to my lovely children Nicholas, Ben and Kate, without whose inadequacies there wouldn't have been a book!

CONTENTS

PREFACE FOR PARENTS

If you are aged 18 or under, you can skip this preface for parents. You can ignore all their insecurities about you leaving home and jump straight to the next section, which is addressed to you.

Dear Parents,

THERE ARE A BILLION THINGS MY 15 YEAR OLD CAN DO. Most of them involve sitting in front of a screen. His imagination can run riot in a parallel universe. But when it comes to this world, just how well equipped is he to cope?

I started writing a list of the practical things I thought he should know how to do and was alarmed to realise that he knew very few of them. His meals are put on the table, his laundry is dropped on the floor and reappears magically cleaned and ironed. Pocket money (now more grandly called an allowance) is given and taken away to produce the odd job completed under duress. Nicholas is astonishingly computer literate but I'm pretty sure he does not know how to put on the washing machine (or where to find it). He raids the fridge but doesn't know how to cook a basic, cheap meal. His 12-year-old brother Ben tried making his favourite meal of tinned tomato soup with a hard-boiled egg in it. After establishing how to turn on the hob, he heated the soup in a saucepan, then took an egg out of the egg box and dropped it, shell and all, into the soup. Alarm bells rang for me.

As children become teenagers and start the journey to independent living, there are skills that will make them better able to cope. They need to make the transition from being fantastically skilled at spending *your* money to learning to live on a budget and fend for themselves. Most students or earners on starter salaries won't have the funds to buy their way out of a problem. (Or, if they do, it will be with *your* funds.)

This book is a checklist of what every parent should make sure their child knows, from how to look after a bike to how to make a bed. It's a daunting task, trying to equip your child with the resources to cope in an increasingly complex and competitive world. By the time your child is starting to get hormonal and difficult, it can seem overwhelming to think about teaching them anything beyond getting out of bed and not answering back. That's where this book can help. Give your child a copy and see how he or she measures up.

My children
My three children failed lamentably with the quiz on page 16. It made me realise what an uphill task I have ahead of me to try to prepare them for independent living. The older two cope brilliantly with public transport and the challenges thrown at them at secondary school, but suggest they clean a football boot or switch on the dishwasher and a vacant look comes upon them. The littlest, perhaps – I hate to say it – because she is a girl, is probably the most adept on the domestic front. But that's not saying much. So this book has been written not because I am a domestic goddess and have passed all my skills on to my offspring; rather, it has been written out of a sense of personal failure.

What they need to know
The selection of the 101 essential things they need to know is inevitably not scientific or definitive. For example, knowing how to construct a sensible letter of complaint or thanks isn't crucial to setting up independently but it is a basic skill that is sensibly acquired in your teens. When I talk to people who have left home, it soon becomes clear that those who had good habits drummed into them as a matter of course were much better able to cope when they found themselves on their own. Self-reliance does not come easily if you have had no training.

When they need to know it
The earlier you start the better. I can say this, having failed on this score with the boys, but I am about to redeem myself with their sister. By the time your child is into double figures they should have acquired a number of the skills in this book and before they get to be intolerably lippy and not listening, they should know most of them. Loading the dishwasher can start from as soon as they are old enough to carry a plate. Teach your child to make their

own sandwiches **when they are 7.** They can learn to use a serious knife sensibly then. They can also clear up when they have finished. **By 10** they should be helping you change their sheets, able to deal with a hot kettle and capable of making cheese on toast. **By 12** they should be able to cook a meal for the household and do basic domestic tasks that require a screwdriver. Putting pictures up, changing light bulbs and cleaning out the U bend ... all these can be accomplished by children reaching their **13th birthday.** They should know about safe sex by then and personal hygiene. **By 14** they probably won't get out of bed without a bribe but you shouldn't give up and you should insist they do their share. They need to know that they have responsibilities. Remember, you are not their slave and in the end they will benefit from not being allowed to wallow in a sloth-like torpor while you run around doing everything for them.

Most of us are so busy coping with our own jobs, bringing up the kids the best we can, coping with financial difficulties and trying to have a life that it is easy to forget the basics that it would be good for our children to know. With this book, you (and they) can spot their weak points and fill in the gaps. It's no good expecting them to discover common-sense skills when they leave home at 18, if they haven't developed some of those skills as they grow up at home.

Doing everything for them

I don't believe in blaming the parents for the sins of the children. You can only do your best and you have to let your children make their own mistakes. However, it is the case that if you always put a meal on the table for them and wash their clothes, it's unlikely they will have much of an opportunity to learn how to do these things. At a time when parents are often out at work and time is at a premium and we live on diets of pre-packaged foods, they are not going to be learning kitchen skills the way some may have done in the past. I even suspect that we may sometimes do more for our children today because we feel guilty at not having enough time and we compensate by making everything nice for them. If that's the case in your house, then you need to adopt a cruel to be kind approach and get those tweenies and teenagers off their butts and helping.

Children need to find their own paths in life and make their own choices and their own mistakes. Nevertheless, you don't want to handicap them by not teaching them the basics of day-to-day survival.

So here is a practical, down-to-earth, no-nonsense guide to doing the basics. Each of the 101 things they need to know is addressed directly to your children but there are additional notes and comments for parents throughout the book. These notes and comments are addressed to 'Dear Parents', but they are intended to be read by all those carers with responsibility for children. Get as much of this list as you can under their belts and you can feel you've done your best to set them off on the right road. Mastering the list won't guarantee avoidance of every pitfall of life, not to mention drugs, drink and sex. However, it will help. Even while they are still at home, it might occasionally encourage them to put on the washing or make you a meal. But don't hold your breath.

'I found leaving home really hard. My mum gave up work when I was little. I was very privileged always having her at home; maybe too privileged. I've been quite babied. I was very independent about academic work but I'd never done any mundane work.' ALEXIS, 18

'When I first moved away from home, I got a bank account and I received statements. I couldn't understand why, although I was spending money, the amount in the account just seemed to go up. The statement had switched to a nice red colour.' KIM, 48

You've got to encourage people to take risks and not to take everything the older generation says for granted.

ANTONY GORMLEY, ARTIST

PREFACE FOR TEENAGERS

Dear Fellow Teenager,

I'VE SPENT MY LIFE BEING TOLD WHAT TO DO by my parents and by my teachers and by everyone older than me, and the thought of leaving home is great. My mum is always telling me to wash; or pick up my clothes from the heap on the floor; or to do my homework; or to come home at a decent hour. She can't come into my room without making critical comments. She even tries to improve my school course work. It is the lot of adults to boss around their children and the lot of children to have to put up with it. If you question it, the adults say, 'This is my house and while you're under my roof you'll do things my way.'

Leaving home

I think I'll leave home when I am 18. My mum isn't convinced I'll survive without her. She can't (or doesn't like to) imagine what the state of my room will be in. Frankly, I don't much care. It doesn't bother me now and I don't suppose it will bother me then. She worries too much.

It is true I will want clean clothes (isn't that why I'll come home for the weekend?); I'll want to eat, travel around, manage money and get by. So my mum's written this book to tell me ... and you ... the key things you need to know in advance. She's collected together what she sees as survival skills for teenagers.

Don't think for a moment that I know how to do all the things in the book. The point is, I don't. If I did, I don't suppose she'd be writing it. You may be much more adept in the kitchen than me or have already set up a flourishing business. You may already have had 20 partners or take Ecstasy regularly. If that's the case, some of the things listed here may seem terribly basic, but I'll bet there are others you take for granted because someone else does them for you.

There is still very often a gender split about what things girls and boys know how to do. I can't sew on a button but I think my sister can. I know that's sexist but I can't see myself ever sewing on a button. I'll just have to beg a favour when I need it. I suppose I can always ring home, which will make mum feel needed.

There's never enough money

I'm always complaining that I don't get a big enough allowance. Compared to most of my friends, I get a pittance. I've thought about trying to get a job, but I play football on Saturdays, so it is a bit limiting. So whenever I want something, I do have to negotiate for it. I always feel short of cash. However, from what I read about university and fees, and then about mortgages and the problems first-time buyers have, I'm only going to get poorer. I certainly won't have much cash to throw around. Unless you are particularly privileged or mollycoddled by your parents you are unlikely to have much cash for a while to throw at anything.

I have come round to mum's way of thinking: that it's much easier to be economical if you have a few basic skills. (She is paying me to write this after all.) It's got to be cheaper to cook a few meals than it is to buy pre-packaged. I even recognise it's cheaper to fix the hem on your own jeans rather than send them to be repaired (but I may just have to save up for that one).

Knowing how to cook

Mum says when she was at university, the best thing she had was a set of 20 porcelain plates she had carried back one holiday from Limoges. She used to feed all her friends spaghetti on them. She's still feeding everyone spaghetti on them. Her repertoire has increased a bit. But she's right that it's good to be able to be sociable on the cheap. I can rustle up a bacon sandwich and I'm very good at opening tins and packets.

Thinking ahead

Mum is one of those people who always like to prepare ahead. She got it from my grandma, who always packs suitcases at least five weeks in advance and worries about next term's school uniform at the beginning of each holiday. I tend to be more of a last-minute person, which drives them both nuts. Mum says when you leave home it's too late to start worrying about what you know and what you don't. I am a late convert to this one. Aged 16 to 18, people have enough to think about, whether it's a new job, a place at college or a gap year abroad. The time to think about whether you are equipped to fly the nest is when you are still in it.

If you think you know it all, prove it. Do the quiz and check your *Fitness to leave home* rating. Whether you're 11 or 17, see how independent you really are and how well you could survive if you were to leave home now. You may be enough of a brain box to appear on *University Challenge*, but can you get rid of a wine stain, clean your shoes and buy a cheap and decent meal? Are you really ready to leave home? I am not prepared to divulge my score. Good luck!

Yours,

Nicholas, 15

ARE THEY READY TO LEAVE HOME?

The quiz that reveals whether they are ready or not

THE QUIZ

Dear Teenager,

SEE HOW MUCH YOU REALLY KNOW by answering the following questions before you read the book. No peeking at the lists or the answers. Write your answers down so there is no nonsense about what you meant to say or nearly said.

NICHOLAS, 15 Or you could just look at the answers and get everything right. In fact, go a step further: look at the answers, make a bet with your parents, then win some money!

QUESTIONS

1. What does the symbol Ⓟ mean on a label?

2. How often should you change your sheets?

3. How much does a pint of milk cost?

4. How do you clean the toilet?

5. How old do you have to be to have a tattoo?

6. You've got guests and you need to provide a meal for four. What are you going to cook?

7. You lose your credit card. What do you do?

8. There is a pile of dirty laundry that needs seeing to. What do you do?

9. What should you do if you had unplanned sex last night?

10. What is the date of your mother's birthday?

ANSWERS *2 points for each answer unless otherwise stated.*

1. Ⓟ is the symbol you find on labels of clothes and means that the item can be dry cleaned (or may be dry clean only). 2 points for the right answer and nothing but the right answer on this one.

2. If you said once a week or once a fortnight, give yourself 2 points. Any less frequently and you probably need to buy an air freshener and be forced to study pictures of bed bugs in large close up.

3. It depends where you live and where you buy it from but if you said between 30 and 40p you get your points. Anything else, no points.

4. Clean the toilet seat with a bathroom cleaner on a cloth. Pour toilet cleaner down the inside and leave. Scrub with toilet brush if necessary. If you were clueless about this one, you should be made to go and clean the toilet right now, and if you are guilty of leaving wee on the seat or not flushing, you should lose 2 points now, irrespective of whether or not you got the answer right.

5. You have to be 18 to have a tattoo.

6. If you can mentally conjure up a simple meal such as pesto pasta with bread and salad or spaghetti Bolognese, give yourself 1 point. If you could write yourself a list of the relevant ingredients, walk into the kitchen and make it, give yourself another point and a Michelin star. If none of the above applies, then go to the **Hungry for Life** section, pronto.

7. Ring your card supplier immediately and cancel it. If you don't, you will be liable for whatever somebody else spends on your card.

8. No, the answer is not 'Give them to your mum' (lose 2 extra points). First separate your clothes into whites and coloureds. Wash them separately in the machine on the appropriate wash cycle. 2 points for the correct answer.

9. If a girl has had unprotected sex and does not want to be pregnant, she can get the morning-after pill from the chemist. It can be used up to 72 hours after sex though with decreasing effectiveness. It is most effective within 24 hours. Give yourself 1 point for the pill and 1 point for the time-frame.

10. 2 points for the right answer, none for anything else, not even if you're close. If you didn't know, you have no idea of what's important in life.

The scoring system

Each question in this quiz scores 2 points, and some are generous enough to offer 1 point for getting close to the answer. Only written answers accepted and no late changes allowed.

Teenagers: There are a possible 20 points. Add up your total and see how prepared you are to leave home.

If you scored really low, you shouldn't be given the choice to leave home; you should probably be thrown out!

16–20: You are too good to be true. You are the perfect teenager who will, in time, develop into a competent, practical young person with a student debt that won't cripple you for more than a decade. In fact you are a bit of a walking miracle. Most reasonably competent adults would find it hard to fall into this Whiz Kid category but you seem to have it all covered from relationship management to domestic know-how. You must be a shining credit to your parents. You will prove very popular at college with very passable social skills. There's even the long-term prospect that you'll look after your parents in their old age. You are a Seriously Good Prospect.

NICHOLAS, 15: So you took my advice and cheated. Congratulations.

8–15: You are a typical, lazy teenager who takes your parents for granted. Your room is probably a tip and washing is something that someone else does. You are, in fact, a completely standard adolescent. You are heading for trouble and you don't care. If you're lucky, your parents won't want you to suffer so they'll end up subsidising you when you run into debt again and again, and they'll kick themselves for not getting your skills up to scratch when you were young enough for them to make you (and shorter than them; it's always harder trying to be authoritative looking upwards). Parents need to get you into remedial training using this book now.

NICHOLAS, 15: Hmm ... I suppose you didn't do badly... If you cheated, you haven't got a very good memory.

0–7: Well, you have a serious problem on your hands. You may be your parents' little darling but you are thoroughly incompetent and expect life to be handed to you on a plate. Your parents' plate. If they're not careful, you will never move out and they'll have a life sentence picking up your dirty washing off the floor. You need to act now or you are in for mayhem and grief. This is an emergency case. Take a dose of this book every day and hope the medicine works.

NICHOLAS, 15: I warned you about being honest. It doesn't work. Now look, someone will be getting you to wash up tonight, and cook tomorrow. And it's all for 'when you go to university'. Maybe now is the time to start saying you have no intention of going to university and remember that, in some European countries, lots of children stay living at home. Remind your parents of the joy of the extended family. That will get them really worried.

STEPPING OUT IN STYLE

YOU MAY BE HAPPY WITH A GRUNGE LOOK but most people don't actually want to smell of stinky feet or sweat. Clothes that are looked after also last longer so for your own sake and that of the person sitting next to you, it would be good to learn to wash and look after your clothes.

Remember too that machines need looking after. Drying machines may need de-fluffing. Washing machines break down when they get coins from your jeans pockets stuck in the works so empty your pockets before you stick your clothes in the machine or basket. Respect the machine as you would your stereo or computer and it's much more likely to stay working for you.

MINI QUIZ

Have your parents trailed around after you doing everything for you or have you learnt how to look after yourself?

1. What does this symbol mean? ⊠
2. How do you wash trainers?
3. Do you know how to work the washing machine?
4. Do you automatically empty your pockets before putting clothes in the washing basket?

Answers

1. Don't put this item in the tumble dryer.
2. Put them inside a pillow case, tie it up and wash in the machine.
3. Hmmmm. Say no more.
4. If the answer is no, you should be billed for all the repair costs.

Dear Teenager,
I HOW TO DO THE WASHING

- First and foremost, empty your pockets. Remove the sweet wrappers, the coins and the paper clips. Take off any belts with buckles that will clank around the machine.

- Now look at the washing labels. Each item you buy has a coded label, which explains how to look after it. It is very simple to decipher. It's a good idea to look at the label in the shop before you buy because if it requires dry cleaning that means you may have to pay to have it cleaned every time you wear it.

- Do not squeeze all you can into the washing machine. Overfilled machines lead to clothes and sheets gummed up with washing powder. Make sure there is room for the contents to move around.

- Coloured clothes should be washed separately from whites. If you don't do this your white clothes will pick up the colours and turn an attractive grey hue.

- You need washing powder or a washing powder cube or gel. It doesn't matter which. Some machines require you to pour the powder into a drawer. Alternatively (and this is easier), use a cube, which you put into the little net that comes with it (or in the drawer – read the box), and pop it into the machine with your washing. The gels are easier still. They just get thrown in with the washing. Don't overdo the quantity. One gel or cube is usually enough.

- You don't need to use fabric conditioner, which is designed to make the clothes softer to the touch. It's not for the uninitiated.

- You can choose either biological or non-biological washing powders. Biological ones contain enzymes which break down stains; non-bio ones are better for sensitive skins. I use non-bio.

- You need to choose a washing cycle. For most things I'd recommend 40 degrees. If you have nice wool jumpers or silks or anything delicate, think about hand washing or dry cleaning. If you do want to try them in the machine, look for a cycle for delicates.

LAUNDRY LANGUAGE
Do you know the meaning of the following symbols?

 This is the temperature at which you need to wash the item in the machine.

 This is for hand washing only. You need to buy a special detergent and wash the item in the sink.

This can go to the dry cleaners. If it's dry clean only, it won't be cheap. Bad luck.

● If you haven't got access to a washing machine, you can go to the launderette. You can take washing powder with you or buy it there. Usually you cannot use the dryers unless you have used the washing machines. It can be quite sociable and warm sitting in the launderette but if you don't fancy it and you have the cash to spare, you can ask for a service wash. You leave your bin bag of washing with the attendant and come and collect it later.

● If you are washing an item like a football shirt that has numbers, letters or designs stuck on to it, wash it inside out. This stops bits from peeling off so quickly.

'Leaving home sounds great. It means being able to do whatever you want with your parents giving you money. It means going clubbing on a Saturday night and coming home late … and on a Friday night too if you have enough money.' NICHOLAS, 15
Q. 'Who will do your washing?' MUM
A. *'I'll send it home to you.'* NICHOLAS, 15

'Washing clothes was a real hassle. When I went to university I managed to go the first nine weeks without washing anything. It was pretty disgusting. I'm not proud of it. I had all my clothes with me. I got a rotation thing going. In my halls, they didn't provide enough laundry facili-

ties. You had to queue for hours to get a machine. In the end I set my alarm very early on a Sunday morning to get a free machine.' ED, 21

'In the first two weeks of being away from home, I learnt lots that I'd never thought about before. For example, I wish I had known the difference between fabric conditioner and washing powder. If only someone had told me. I also wish I'd known that you don't wash wool on a hot cycle before all my jumpers came out very small.' TIAN, 20

'I'd never done any washing before. Well, on holiday I'd rinsed out a bikini in the sink but I'd never used an actual washing machine. I thought I'd be the only one like that but in fact I found lots of people were the same.' ALEXIS, 18

'I'm terrible at washing. I had this theory that the more powder you put in, the cleaner your clothes got. It's not true. It just makes them harder.' GEORGE, 20

Dear Teenager,
2 HOW TO DRY YOUR CLOTHES
The best advice about the tumble dryer or drying machine is to try not to use it. It's expensive to run (it really ups your electricity bill) and can shrink your clothes.

- Best of all, if the weather is OK, hang your washing out on a line. The pegs are probably kept near the washing machine. Clothes always smell and feel best when they have dried outside.

- If you haven't got a garden, or it's raining, hang your clothes over the back of a chair (or a clothes horse if you have one).

- Dresses, shirts and trousers can be hung on clothes hangers. Twist the wire handle and stick the hanger over the top of a door. Your clothes will need less (or no) ironing if you treat them well at this stage.

- Radiators are best avoided. They are OK if you need to dry some socks in a hurry but things left on them tend to wrinkle and shrivel. Covering some radiators that need to be kept clear can be dangerous.

- At the end of its drying programme, the drying machine runs on cold for 10 minutes. You should let it run its course because it can damage the machine to stop it sooner.

- Do not leave things lying in the drying machine for hours. They will crease horribly. Take them out and hang them up as soon as the machine stops.

- Whatever you do, don't follow the advice of either Alexis or George under any circumstances!

'I don't use the drying machines. I use a hair dryer. It works very well. My clothes are small so they get dry quickly.' ALEXIS, 18

'We have little, tiny rooms like prison cells so I nail my clothes with drawing pins to the walls. I did leave them in a wet heap a couple of times but they just started to smell.' GEORGE, 20

'My mum is Afro-Caribbean and my dad's Jamaican. There's always been a strong tradition in our culture that as soon as you can do stuff, you do it. It's not, "Would you... ?" You just do.' KACHENGA, 19

SHRINK DRY

If you do use a tumble dryer, either at home or at a launderette, check the labels on your garments first. Not everything can be put in a drying machine. A rule of thumb is that anything stretchy or delicate shouldn't go in.

This symbol means it is OK to put it in the machine.

 This symbol means you must not put it in the machine.

I'm a great believer that in an emergency you can do anything so long as you lower your standards. You can do anything if you just commit to doing it. I have often worn wet things to weddings and auditions. You wash them at the last minute and they're still not dry. Just put them on and they'll dry!

FIONA SHAW,
ACTRESS (AUNT
PETUNIA IN THE *HARRY
POTTER* FILMS)

Dear Teenager,
3 HOW TO HANG UP YOUR CLOTHES

In my house anyone who gets undressed seems congenitally incapable of moving their trousers an inch beyond where they have dropped round their ankles. Dirty clothes and clean are of course mixed together and, without my intervention, the clothes pile would just become a clothes mountain. If you are the person doing the washing, this is intolerable.

At some point in life the person responsible for your washing is likely to be you. You are also likely to be living on a restricted income and will not have endless new clothes. So you need to look after the ones that you've got, and you need to be able to find them. You need some sort of order.

● When you get undressed, separate the dirty clothes from the clean and put the dirty in a washing bag or basket. Pick up shirts or jackets or jumpers to be re-worn and put the shoulders on to a hanger. Hang up.

● Organise your storage space so that you can find things easily. Pants and socks go in the top drawer. Tee-shirts and tops go in the next. Trousers go in the bottom drawer. The more you can hang up dresses, skirts, trousers, shirts, the better. They will be more visible and they will crease less so you'll have to do less ironing.

29

A HANGER?

MY clothes..?

on a HANGER?

● It's a good idea to sort out your wardrobe or drawers by empty-
ing them out altogether. Only put back in what you really need and
wear. You're allowed to keep one old pair of trousers for painting
and gardening but otherwise anything you haven't worn in a year
but is still in good shape should go to the charity shop for recycling. You don't need it and you won't miss it. Kiss it goodbye.

*'When it comes to hanging things up I tend to find it easier to throw
the clothes on the floor and hope they get picked up by someone else.
After all, what are parents for?'* NICHOLAS, 15

*'Lots of my friends have two piles of clothes in their room. One clean;
one dirty.'* TIAN, 20

*'I still don't hang up my clothes. It's worse than washing. For the first
term I lived out of my suitcase. Now I fold things up in drawers. I
change about four times a day and hanging clothes up seems so time-
consuming.'* ALEXIS, 18

*'I wasn't at all house-trained. We had a washing basket at home but I
ignored it. I dropped my clothes in my room. Every so often mum came
in and picked up a pile of mouldy clothes and they reappeared in my
cupboard.'* OLLIE, 18

Dear Teenager,
4 HOW TO CLEAN SHOES

If you were to join the army, you would be taught to clean your boots
meticulously and regularly. For those of you with no intention of
signing up, you can probably get by with more of a spit and a polish. However, having once seen a soldier on a train journey, cleaning his boots for an hour with a toothbrush, I can report that the
activity looked curiously satisfying. The soldier told me he had
owned and worn the same pair of boots for 14 years.

● **Trainers:** If you wear trainers, the best way to clean them is to put
them in a pillowcase, tie a knot in the pillowcase to keep them inside,
and throw them in the washing machine on a 40-degree cycle. Most

manufacturers will not recommend this so you are taking a risk, but it's worked every time for me. Alternatively, you can slave away with a whitener, but they won't ever look like new again.

● **Leather shoes:** For leather shoes, there is nothing better than elbow grease. First get yourself some newspaper. This is a messy process so be warned and don't do it without paper on the kitchen surface where you prepare food. Get a cloth or a brush, put on the polish (neutral, brown or black), leave it for ten minutes, then rub off with a clean cloth or brush and consider signing up. Your grandparents' generation did National Service and lived at a time when clothing was rationed so they are accustomed to caring for their shoe leather. They would surely disapprove of the instant shoe shine you can buy, which you simply rub on and leave. It's not as effective but it's better than nothing, and it's clean and quick to use. Don't leave leather shoes on a radiator to dry or they will be ruined.

● **Football boots:** Football boots are disgusting objects. From the moment they walk off the pitch, and particularly in winter, they always manage to bring all the mud of the field back with them. Before you get in a car or step inside a house, remove the boots and beat them together with passion. Do not do this outside someone's front gate so that they walk out into a mud bath. Once home, stand over a newspaper or a bin or in the garden, and scrape off the big dollops of mud with an old knife. Then run the underside of the boots under the tap and clean off the rest with your fingers. Stuff the boots with clean newspaper and leave to dry. Wash the sink and knife thoroughly with disinfectant, clean up any other debris, then go and have a well-deserved shower.

'I'm probably unusual in this. I go hiking a lot and hiking equipment is expensive. If it's expensive, you look after it.' TIAN, 20

'I never clean shoes. I wear trainers and as soon as they get dirty, I buy another pair.' KACHENGA, 19

Dear Teenager,
5 HOW TO IRON A SHIRT

You can get away without ironing a lot of things. If you are certain you are going to be wearing a jumper, you only need to iron the shirt collar (but it does rather spoil the impression if the temperature goes up and you are forced to cast off the jumper). Before you grab an iron, check the garment label first.

Ironing tips

● It is easier to iron things that are slightly damp rather than bone dry.

● Always iron on a board with an ironing cover or on a very large clear surface covered in towels.

● If you have an instruction book with your iron, check whether it prefers distilled or ordinary water. Spraying water from the iron as you go can help eliminate stubborn creases.

● Never, ever, leave the iron unattended, not even to answer the door or the phone.

● If you are ironing cotton you can have a hot iron. If you are ironing delicate or polyester fabrics you need a much cooler iron. If you have clothes with transfers on them, iron them inside out. For very delicate fabrics or things you are not sure about, place a damp, clean tea-towel on top of the item and iron on top of that.

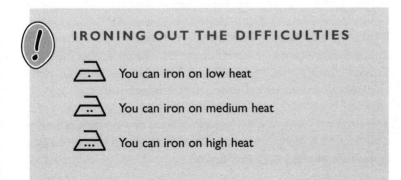

IRONING OUT THE DIFFICULTIES

You can iron on low heat

You can iron on medium heat

You can iron on high heat

● Let the iron cool down before you put it away.

Ironing strategy for shirts

It is a good thing to learn how to iron a shirt. It is easier if you start with the shirt slightly damp, so as not to fight the creases from the washing machine.

● Start with the collar, then the nape (that's the panel between the shoulders).

● Next, iron the sleeves.

● Then iron the back of the shirt, spreading it over the ironing board so you have the maximum surface area to iron.

● Last of all, iron the two front pieces with the buttons and but-tonholes. This is the bit that's most on view so should be tackled last and made as smooth as possible.

Packing strategy for shirts

If you are sticking a shirt in a bag and want it to look presentable when you take it out, here's what to do.

● Button up the (ironed) shirt.
● Lay the shirt, front down, on a table or bed.
● Fold one side into the centre, then the other side.
● Lift a sleeve and fold it so that it lies smoothly down the length of the shirt. Repeat with the other sleeve.
● Fold the shirt in half from the bottom.
● Turn it over and store in a plastic bag.

A friend of mine told me how she was in a hurry to go out and the shirt she was wearing was a bit crumpled. She picked up the iron and ran it over the shirt on her body. Inevitably she burned herself badly. So always remove clothes before ironing them!

'I used to wear my clothes for a couple of hours and the creases would disappear. Now I've got an ironing board. If I'm going out and I want to make an impression, I'll iron.' ED, 21

'I haven't got an iron yet. I can't be bothered to go and get one. There is one in the halls of residence but it's used for antics, not ironing'. TIAN, 20

'None of my clothes are good enough to be ironed.' IAN, 19

'I iron quite well. I like seeing a crumpled shirt turn to perfection. The reward is immediate.' KACHENGA, 19

Dear Teenager,
6 HOW TO SEW ON A BUTTON
(and other useful sewing tips)

This is a skill that is easier than you can imagine and yet some people go through their lives never doing it and maintaining that they can't. Usually when people do that, it's job avoidance. But actually the time they spend pleading with someone else to do them this favour and promising rewards would be more productively spent sewing the button on in the first place.

- First find some thread. Ideally it should be the same colour as the garment from which the button came. Cut the thread to about 40 cm long. Too long and it gets all knotted, too short and you can't do the job properly.

- Thread a needle, which is best done by licking the end of the thread so that it passes easily through the eye of the needle. Pull the two ends of the thread to the same length. You are almost there, and if you carry on like this you will soon be making your own clothes.

- On the spot where the button needs to be attached, pass the needle down and up through the fabric, leaving about 2 cm of thread visible on the top. Repeat, this time pulling the thread gently through all the way. Repeat.

- Now it's time to push the needle up through one of the holes in the button. Pass the needle down through another hole in the button and through the fabric to the other side. Then bring the needle up through the fabric and through another hole in the button.

Repeat at least four times.

● Now your button is secure and you need to knot the thread by sewing a couple of stitches on top of one another on the reverse side of the fabric. Cut off the thread and any other thread that is showing. Some buttons have a loop rather than holes, but the same principles apply.

You may find that you have pricked your fingers several times. This is why real seamstresses wear thimbles, but I think you'll just have to put up with it. After all, no gain without pain.

'I can't do this. Just can't. It's all too small. And the needle hurts when it pricks you. You can end up with blood on your clothes instead of a button. This is when you have to resort to a charm offensive, and persuade someone else to do it for you. Nice to make other people feel needed.' NICHOLAS, 15

'The mum of an old boyfriend of mine had a really good idea. It was a Useful Box. It was full of pins and needles and Sellotape and all the things you don't realise you constantly need until you don't have them. At home they're always around and when you leave home you suddenly need them.' MATILDA, 20

'I've never attempted it. If I needed to do it, I'd probably go to my friend Izzy who is a domestic goddess. She helps out lots of people.' ALEXIS, 18

'I can do this. I used to make my own clothes. I went through a punk phase and I couldn't find trousers that were baggy enough so I made them.' WILL, 18

Dear Parents,

Just think about all those name tags that had to be sewn on to their clothes when they were younger. You could have got them to sharpen up their sewing skills by giving them the job. So if they have any younger siblings, now's your chance. Just hand them the sewing box now!

HOUSE TRAINING

THESE ARE THE SKILLS YOU NEED TO SURVIVE around the house. They are very useful while you're living at home because you can easily butter up parents by doing any of them. Sometimes teenagers seem pathetically slow at picking up the message that if they are seen to be helpful, they usually reap rewards. (I don't mean straight bribes here, just that an adult's mood is always softened when someone else has done the clearing up.) And they are useful when you are finally let loose on your own.

Cleaning generally may seem a hideously boring subject. I don't mind cleaning my body but I'm pretty averse to cleaning houses. Equally, I'm not that keen on living in a pigsty and not being able to find anything. One trick is to de-clutter and throw out what you don't need. Another is to have a regular home for regularly used objects. You're more likely to be able to find your football shorts or your CD or your paper supply if you put them back in the same place each time. The object is to cut out unnecessary work and make life easier.

MINI QUIZ

Are you squeaky clean and houseproud or a dirty layabout?

1. When did you last use the vacuum cleaner?
2. How many bed mites are there in the average mattress?
3. If someone impartial made an inspection of your room, what would they make of the state of it?

Answers

1. What does this say about you?
2. Between 100 thousand and 10 million.
3. Congratulations if your room passes muster. Commiserations to your mother if it doesn't.

Dear Teenager,
7 HOW TO WASH AND DRY UP

I once stayed at a friend's house where the washing up was a work of art. All the dirty plates and glasses were neatly arranged; the knives and forks were lined up and the washing up looked as if it had been done before it had been started. It was impressive. I'm not quite that orderly but a bit of planning does help.

- It's useful to equip yourself with a washing up bowl (or a plug for the sink); a clean washing up cloth; a pad or a brush for tough grime; washing up liquid; an apron to stop you ruining your clothes; and, if you want to protect your hands, a pair of rubber gloves.

- Always wash up in hot, soapy water. It's a lot more effective than cold or tepid or just running an object under a tap.

- Wash your glasses first. They are likely to be least dirty and you don't want to be washing them in the remains of your stew.

- Leave heavily soiled pans or baking trays to soak in hot water and washing up liquid. It takes longer but it is a lot easier in the long run.

- It's a good idea to rinse things in clean hot water (either under the tap or in a second sink if you have the luxury) to get rid of the washing up liquid, before placing them on the draining board.

- When you have finished, wash the sink down and spray with an antibacterial cleaner.

Parents frequently ask their offspring to do the drying up, largely because it seems like a relatively safe activity and doesn't involve much instruction or telling off. My view, however, is that whenever possible, the drying up should not be done at all. It is often an unhygienic activity that is a waste of time. After all, the dishes will get dry without you interfering.

On the other hand, it sometimes has to be done because there is too much of it in too crowded a space. In this case, if asked, you could agree to do it just to look willing.

● You should insist on using a clean tea towel. Bacteria grow in damp cloths and all you'll be doing is spreading infection if you use a wet or dirty one. Once used, stick it in the wash.

● Do not use the tea towel to wipe up spills on the floor or use it instead of oven gloves, thus covering it in bits of food. Do not use it for drying your hands when you have been to the loo. In fact use it as little as possible and know that all the world's top hygienists are right behind you.

● If you have fancy glasses, you could dry these because undried glasses sometimes have staining on them. I'm not fussed about this but you may be and the superior way of dealing with them is with a very hygienic paper towel.

The main benefit of drying up is a social one. It's a very good opportunity to have a chat in a non-confrontational way with the person doing the washing up. So if you have to do the drying up, make the most of it.

'According to a report I found on the internet, nine out of ten dishcloths used to clean kitchens in restaurants hold potentially infectious bugs, such as salmonella and E coli. So if you don't want vomiting and stomach cramps, say "No" to drying up.' NICHOLAS, 15

Dear Teenager,
8 HOW TO LOAD AND UNLOAD THE DISHWASHER

The dishwasher is usually white (or stainless steel if you are posh) and placed discreetly near the sink. Consider yourself lucky if you have one. It's very speedy to load and unload and you gain enormously in popularity if you take on the task.

Some people are particularly anal about their dishwasher and put all their forks into one section and their knives into another. Feel sorry for these people. You are not meant to be a slave to the machine, it's meant to make your life easier. These are the simple dishwasher rules.

● If your dishes are very dirty, rinse them under the tap first instead of clogging up the dishwasher with baked beans or leftover veg.

● Arrange the dishes in an orderly fashion. If you pack them in too closely they will come out dirty and you'll get stuck with washing them by hand.

● Forks and spoons go in the cutlery holder head up, but put knives in blade down so you don't cut yourself when you retrieve them.

● If things persist in coming out mucky, put some rinse aid into the machine as well as some dishwasher salt. There is a hole for each, and both these products can be purchased at the supermarket.

● There is normally a basic programme to set the dishwasher and this is the one to go for rather than pre-washes or anything more complicated.

● You will get brownie points, when the wash is done, if you unload the dishwasher, which takes less than five minutes. Try not to say 'Where does this go?' about everything that you take out. You can probably have a good guess.

'I don't unpack. There's no need. You can just take what you want from the machine when you need it.' NICHOLAS, 15

'If you flat share, you'll find a few people are housetrained and you pick up tips from them.' OLLIE, 18

Dear Teenager,
9 HOW TO PREVENT A KITCHEN FIRE

Every day 20 people are killed or injured in kitchen fires in the UK. In the kitchen you're dealing with a highly combustible mix of gas, electricity and grease, and we are often too casual about it. The first thing you should check is that you have a working smoke alarm, not in the kitchen where it will go off all the time, but in the hall-way outside. Unless it's wired into your electric circuit, you need to check the battery regularly. Accidental house fires frequently occur in homes where there are alarms fitted, but the batteries are dead. If you are in rented accommodation and you don't have a smoke alarm, take it up with the landlord.

Another piece of good safety equipment is a fire blanket. This can be wrapped around someone whose clothing catches fire. It can also be draped over a pan that catches fire on the hob.

The rest is down to you acquiring sensible habits.

- Keep the hob and oven clean. A build-up of grease is highly flam-mable so fire will take hold much more quickly.

- Make sure your toaster is not situated near to curtains or rolls of paper towels.

- If you need to light your hob manually, buy a spark device. It's much safer than matches.

- When you are cooking, always make sure the pan handle is not sticking out.

- Always hold the handle with one hand and stir with the other.

- Never leave a pan unattended on the hob, not even to nip off to answer your phone. It's astonishingly easy to forget it.

- Keep drying up cloths and electrical leads well away from the cooker. Use a flame-proof oven glove rather than a tea towel to move hot pots and pans.

- Keep a fire blanket in an accessible place in your kitchen.

 Most kitchen fires occur between 10 p.m. and 4 a.m., presumably when people are tired or have been drinking.

FIRE FIGHTING
If there is a fire on the stove, here is what to do.

● If you have a fire blanket, cover the flaming pan with it.

● If you can, turn off the heat. Leave the pan to cool.

● If you do not have a fire blanket, wet a cloth under the tap, wring it out and cover the pan. Never throw water over it.

● If you can't put the fire out, shut the kitchen door, get our of the house and call 999.

● Never deep-fat fry in an open pan. It is just too dangerous. If you want to do this, invest in a special, enclosed deep-fat fryer.

● Don't overload your kitchen electrics. Washing machines need their own sockets. If you are using several appliances via a fused bar adaptor, check the total number of amps is no more than 13.

'My dad taught me to cook. Some of my friends didn't know the first thing about cooking and have done some really stupid things. Like my flat-mate who tried cooking beans in a plastic container, which he put on the hob. And then put a red-hot frying pan on a plastic chopping board and melted it. Mind you, we're still using the chopping board.' ED, 21

'It's not as difficult as I thought it would be. I've become much more confident in the kitchen. I've got burnt a few times but that's all part of learning on the job.' IAN, 19

 www.firekills.gov.uk tells you how to prevent fires and what to do in an emergency.

Dear Teenager,
10 HOW TO CLEAN YOUR ROOM

Boring, boring, boring. What's the point anyway? Well your parents would probably say while you're in their house you should at least try not to treat it like a pigsty, and what about the things they have bought you, which you are now treating like junk? But that's between you and your parents.

There may come a time, however, when you live somewhere else. Maybe then your flatmates will want to evict you because the smell of unwashed socks and pizza boxes is overwhelming them. Or maybe you will decide you want to be a reformed character in order to be able to have people round without asphyxiating them. So where do you start?

● Open a window if you can. A little fresh air can do a lot of good.

● Get a large black dustbin bag and throw everything away that you possibly can.

● Collect all dirty washing and wash. Ditto with crockery, glasses, pots, pans and empty bottles and cans.

● Put everything away in a suitable space. This does not mean cramming everything behind a cupboard door or under the bed. If it hasn't got a home, you should probably junk it. Move the bed so you can see all the way underneath it.

● Completely clear all surfaces of books, magazines and accumulated rubbish. Wipe non-wooden surfaces with a duster to remove dust and dirt. For wooden surfaces spray with polish then wipe with a duster. If you have to, put the objects back onto your nice, shiny surfaces. Better still, bin them.

● Sweep, using a broom and a dustpan. Or vacuum if you have a carpet. You will feel like a new person and you will be in control of your space. You'll probably also find a few items that went missing years ago.

● Remember to recycle as much as you can (see **How to Recycle**).

When you live in a shared flat, the question of who does the cleaning is often a hot issue. Some people don't see mess; others can't abide it. Willingness to pick up a broom and knowledge of where the bin bags live strike me as basics for successful communal living.

'My mum comes down to my room and starts to tidy it. I tell her not to, but she does it all the same. Then she gets upset and asks why there are so many papers everywhere and why can't I file them? I know exactly where everything is, until she comes along and moves it all. I think somebody's room is their business. It's my mess and I like it.'
NICHOLAS, 15

'The biggest issue in our flat is when to take the rubbish out. Mostly people don't even know how to tie up the tie-handles of the bags and they get filled too full. We have a tiny kitchen and there are always three big bags waiting to go out, which contain lots of empty alcohol bottles that stink the place out.' MATILDA, 20

'I lived in a flat with one girl and three boys. It's much harder than you think. The smallest things start to annoy you, like people not putting the lids back on jars. People, especially boys, can be really inconsiderate, especially regarding cleanliness.' ANNA, 24

'Cleaning is one of the things we're going to have to work out when five of us move into a flat together. We'll need a rota set in stone so that people don't pass the buck.' OLLIE, 18

Dear Parents,

The bedrooms of teenagers are nearly always disgusting. I guess it is part of the process of teenage rebellion and desire to test the limits, combined with adolescent sloth. The rooms of teenage boys in particular (and I have this on good authority from several friends) always smell. I don't know whether they are conditioned biologically to fart a lot while they are growing. I suggest lavender air spray, and lots of open windows and closed doors. Just remember, they will be moving away before long and you might even miss them.

'My room is renowned for being messy. I understand my mess, it's logical. But it doesn't look very pleasant. My mum is incredibly tidy. I don't let her see my room in term time.' ALEXIS, 18

Dear Teenager,
11 HOW TO CHANGE THE BED

Changing your bed is a good thing and a very desirable thing, especially if you have any intention of sharing it with someone else.

Squeaky clean people change their sheets once a week. I think every fortnight is perfectly adequate. Some people leave their beds to fester for months. Take a look at what's on the sheets, both that which is visible to the naked eye and that which is only visible with a microscope, and you might think the festering option is not so cool. Ten per cent of the weight of a two-year-old pillow can be composed of dead bed mites and their droppings.

- Use a pillow protector. This can be specially bought. Or use two pillowcases on top of each other. The debris and grease left by your head and hair is considerable and after only a few weeks the pillow can become quite nasty, unless protected.

- Use a mattress protector if you can afford one. Otherwise cover the mattress with an old blanket. This will help keep the mattress cleaner and is probably more hygienic for you if you're sleeping in an ancient bed.

- Experts say you should turn your mattress over every month and vacuum it to shift those bed mites. That's admirable but I can't say I remember to do it that often. Do turn it from time to time, especially if you have a dodgy old mattress.

- If you have a duvet, bed changing is quite straightforward. Remove the sheet, duvet and pillowcase and take to the washing machine.

- Wash, dry and iron them (check out the **Stepping Out in Style** section). Do not put the sheets back on the bed until they are properly dry.

45

AND SO TO BED...
How to put a duvet into a duvet cover.

If you don't approach it the right way, putting a duvet cover on a duvet can end up like trying to wind a toga around yourself. Hold the bottom left-hand corner of the duvet and shove it inside the duvet cover, not letting go until you have inserted it in the left-hand corner of the cover. Put the bottom right-hand corner of the duvet into the bottom right corner of the cover. Pick up the duvet and cover from the bottom corners and shake the rest of the cover into place.

● If you have old-fashioned sheets and blankets you have to work a bit harder. You can try for hospital corners but maybe you should stop short of perfect and settle for being neat, clean and organised. When you can, leave your covers pulled back so that the bed can air.

The idea of changing the bed feels a bit unrewarding but in fact the feel of clean sheets is lovely and may contribute to you sleeping well. Sweet dreams.

'My boyfriend's mum folds his bedclothes, puts a hot water bottle in his bed and makes him a packed lunch. It's going to be a bit of a change when he moves away from home....' JOCASTA, 18

'My mum always enforced the two-week rule at home and I have carried on with it. My mate doesn't. I know for a fact he didn't know how to change his duvet, so he just stuck the duvet cover on the top like a blanket.' TIAN, 20

'I change my sheets once a week and Hoover the floor. One of my flatmates is really bad. His room is foul!' IAN, 19

Dear Teenager,
12 HOW TO CLEAN THE TOILET

This is one of life's great undesirables, but it has to be faced. I know someone who employed a cleaning lady who would do everything except clean the loos. I wouldn't have employed her. You can't start getting precious about dirt that's all right to deal with and dirt that isn't.

Toilets in houses with boys in them are always pretty horrid. Not being a boy, it's hard for me to be sympathetic or understanding about why it's so hard to pee into the bowl. But even the toilet used in the most ladylike way still needs to be cleaned regularly. My mum is a demon cleaner and we've debated long and hard the best way of cleaning a toilet. This is her final judgement.

- First put on a pair of rubber gloves. Next get a bucket of warm water. Squeeze in an all-purpose cleaner. Using a cloth dipped in the bucket, clean around the lid, the seat and then the outside of the bowl, removing all the muck.

- Tip your bucket of soapy water down the loo. Using the toilet brush, scrub the inside of the bowl. Then flush.

- Pour some bleach down the toilet (look for an environmentally friendly one) and leave it unflushed for several hours. This gets rid of staining on the porcelain.

- Wash your gloves and put them away for next time. Throw away the cloth. Admire your sparkling loo.

One extra word of advice: assuming you're not playing Mrs Mop every day, it is a good idea to have a packet of antiseptic wipes near the loo, which can always be used to wipe down the seat (but throw them away, don't flush them down the toilet).

'The toilet? You just don't clean it. You learn to live in a non-clean environment because nobody wants to do it. You just have to spend as little time as possible in the bathroom.' MATILDA, 20

'The toilet question is a sore point. We clean it, reluctantly. It's the one thing that people tend to think you can leave because it gets dirty anyhow. But it's probably the most unhygienic place. No one wants to clean the floor around it. We've got into better habits now.' ED, 21

'The toilet? No, guys don't. It's a taboo subject. But I buy a bottle of bleach from Tesco each month.' TIAN, 20

'We have a cleaner!' IAN, 19

> Many years ago my mum came to stay with me in London. She said she was going to take a bath. She went into the bathroom, came out and said she'd changed her mind. Always clean the bathroom if your mum is coming to stay.
>
> FIONA SHAW, ACTRESS
> (AUNT PETUNIA IN THE *HARRY POTTER* FILMS)

Dear Teenager,
13 HOW TO UNBLOCK A SINK

There is nothing more irritating than having to ring up a plumber for a blockage. Except perhaps being charged an exorbitant sum for something you could possibly have fixed yourself.

Showers
If the water is not draining away from your shower tray, investigate the drain. Inside it, there should be a tube, which you can twist and remove. You will probably find that it is covered in a giant, greasy hair ball. Simply clean it up and re-insert. You should inspect this each week to avoid a build-up.

Sinks
If the sink isn't draining properly, you can try a plunger (available from hardware shops), which you place over the plug hole and push up and down. If you're lucky, you'll dislodge the blockage and the water flow will start again.

Alternatively, you can buy a solution (from a plumbing shop or DIY centre) that you pour down the sink and leave to work overnight. If you're lucky, this will clear out the blockage. Drain cleaners can be very nasty and you need to follow manufacturer's instructions and handle with real care.

U-bends

Often you simply need to access and clear out the U-bend. The U-bend lives underneath the sink and most of the time you can remain blissfully unaware of it, but then you get a blocked sink or you lose a valuable ring down the sink, and suddenly the U-bend becomes jolly important.

The U-bend is named after its shape. It is there as a net to catch things and it is there to prevent smells from the pipes further down coming back at you. If you need to investigate your U-bend, here's how to do it.

● First clear out the cupboard underneath. Take a bucket or bowl and place it under the U-bend. Carefully unscrew it ... there are usually two screws, one at either side. Water will gush into the bucket as you release it and you will be left with a smelly, greasy, nasty piece of pipework in your hands.

● Once you've located your lost ring or valuable, wash out the pipe in a bucket. Don't just shove all the debris back into the sink you've been clearing out. Stick any gunk in the dustbin and pour the liquid down the drain outside.

● Congratulate yourself. You've just saved yourself a massive call-out fee from a plumber.

'We had a blocked sink. If you call someone out to deal with it, it costs a bomb, so we did the job ourselves. It was a bit hit or miss, with everyone holding bowls under the sink. We did it by trial and error and it was disgustingly full of fat right to the top. You have to learn how to do it or it will cost you.' OLLIE, 18

'I don't even know what a U-bend is!' ALEXIS, 18

Dear Teenager,
14 HOW TO GET RID OF RED
WINE STAINS

So you've had the party, everything's gone swimmingly, nothing's broken, but … there's a huge great red wine stain on the carpet or on the sofa. What do you do?

● Best of all is to act straight away. Don't think, 'I'll leave it until the morning.' Do it now. The best and simplest solution is to mop up the excess with a paper towel (being careful not to scrub) and pour on a heap of table salt. Be generous here, not just a pinch or two. Pour it, go back to your party and, in the morning, Hoover away the salt and all should be just like new.

● Alternatively, some people advocate pouring white wine on to the spill, then mopping up the excess with paper towels. This method seems a bit like pouring good money after bad and I am too mean to have tried it.

● If you've got red wine on your clothing, take it off, sprinkle on the salt, then put the garment in cool water. Do not soak in hot water because this sets the stain. Some people suggest treating the stain with a vinegar solution (three parts water to one part vinegar) or soda water. You can take your pick but without doubt the most effective solution is to act immediately.

● My best advice would be to invest in a specialist red wine stain removal product, available from kitchenware manufacturers, and just keep it handy in a cupboard for when disaster strikes.

'Wine stains on clothes go to the dry cleaners. Wine stains on the carpet? You cover them with a rug.' TIAN, 20

'I lived in Paris for a while and you soon become an expert there on dealing with red wine stains. Salt does the trick.' KACHENGA, 19

Dear Teenager,
15 HOW TO PAINT A ROOM

If you had the skills needed to paper, decorate, rewire and revamp a house, you would be priceless. If that's not your forte, a quick lick of fresh paint in a room can lift the spirits and make your living conditions more agreeable. This could improve your bedroom at home or brighten up digs when you move on.

Paint is surprisingly expensive, but the damage you can do with its contents is infinitely more so. The key to re-painting a room is to do the correct preparation.

● Make sure you are wearing old clothes that can get messed up. Don't wear your best shoes.

● Clear away as much furniture as you can. Anything left in the room should be covered, perhaps with an old sheet. Curtains should be taken down. If you have a carpet that cannot be lifted, cover it carefully with newspaper and tape it down with masking tape. If you end up spilling your paint or even splattering it, you are going to be a lot worse off than when you started.

● Choose a light colour. It brightens a room and you're less likely to make a mistake or tire of it than if you choose fuchsia or olive (or black).

KNOW YOUR PAINTS
Emulsion: water-based paint for walls and ceilings. Comes in three finishes: matt (non-reflective and best at hiding lumps and bumps), satin and silk (both a bit shinier than matt, but each has a subtly different surface sheen).
Kitchen and bathroom paint: moisture-resistant emulsion, better for steamy rooms.
Gloss and eggshell: solvent-based (and smelly) paints traditionally used on wood and metal. Water-based products are more environmentally friendly.
Primer: base coat needed on bare plaster or wood before you paint them for the first time.

TOOLS FOR THE JOB

Paint
Filler for cracks
Brushes
Tray and roller
White spirit
Jam jar
Masking tape
Damp cloth
Old sheets or lots of newspaper

● If you're painting the ceiling, do it first as the paint may run.

● While you work it is good to have a damp cloth handy. It has a thousand uses and when your hands are paint splattered and you think you've got some blobs on the soles of your shoes, you don't want to be running through the house to the kitchen.

● I am assuming you are going to paint over wallpaper or old paint and are not going to do the proper thing and strip it all back. To prepare the walls, look for any nasty glitches and cracks. Smooth the area with sandpaper. Apply filler and, when dry, sand down again. Apply a primer coat and then a top coat, or just two coats of your top coat. You can use a brush or a roller. The trouble with rollers is that they easily splatter paint in the most unexpected directions unless you apply them with real sensitivity.

● If you're going to attempt the woodwork, do it last. Rub down, fill, paint. If you're doing window frames, use tape to mask the panes of glass and if you get paint on the glass, wait until it is dry, then scrape gently with a sharp knife. Windows are difficult, so if you're not confident, give them a miss (maybe try cleaning them instead!) and go for the walls.

● Always clean your brushes well. If you have been using emulsion, you can wash the brushes under the tap. If you have been using gloss, you will need white spirit. This is nasty stuff if it spills. Pour some into an old jam jar and soak your brushes in it.

Now it may not be perfect. You may not be able to reach behind the radiator and there may be a lumpy bit that you couldn't smooth out, but the eye of anyone coming into the room will be taken by the general effect. It's really very easy and satisfying. Now you've finished one room, you'll want to take on another!

Dear Teenager,
16 HOW TO CHANGE A LIGHT
BULB (and other electrical tips)

Electricity is dangerous and if you don't know what you are doing you shouldn't be doing it. Better to pay for a proper electrician. If you take up amateur carpentry you might put a nail through your thumb but the damage is relatively small. You can do far worse to yourself and your property by messing with electricity.

Naturally you should never touch anything electrical with wet hands because water conducts electricity very easily. If someone receives an electric shock, don't touch them or you will get a shock too. Switch off the power supply instead, or drag them away from the source by their clothing.

There are, however, six basic electrical skills that everyone can master safely and that are incredibly useful to know.

● First, know where your consumer unit is. This is usually a white box a bit bigger than a shoe box. It might be in the kitchen, under the stairs or in the garage. It controls the distribution of electricity to all the circuits in the house, and contains a circuit fuse or circuit breaker (a small on-off switch) for each circuit. It is very helpful to label them so you know which fuse or circuit breaker controls which part of the system. If something goes wrong with one of the circuits, you'll find the affected switch in its off position. Simply switch it on. If it flicks off again there is probably something wrong with an appliance. Disconnect all the appliances on the circuit and retry. Older houses may still have a fuse box containing several circuit fuses. If this is the case, a fault may blow a fuse and you will have to call an electrician in to replace it.

● Secondly, know how to change a plug fuse. All new appliances these days come with a plug attached by the manufacturer, so it is not so important to know how to wire a plug. But plug fuses can fail and need replacing. Always replace a fuse with one of the same amp rating as the one that was there before. Unscrew the plug with a screwdriver. Lift out the old fuse and slot in the new one. It really is that simple.

● Thirdly, you know all the jokes about how many people it takes to change a light bulb, but can you actually change one? See below for how to do it.

● Fourthly, keep a supply of light bulbs handy because they always go at awkward moments. You are likely to need screw-cap and bayonet-cap bulbs, in the regular and small sizes, in several different wattages. Usually table lamps require 60-watt bulbs and

HOW TO CHANGE A LIGHT BULB

1. Make sure that the light switch is turned off before you start work.
2. Do not stand on top of a shaky stool or cushions piled high on the sofa. Stand on something appropriate (a step ladder held by someone else or a sturdy four-legged chair).
3. Do not touch a light bulb while it is still hot. Leave it to cool. Remove the old bulb, by pushing it in and turning it anti-clockwise if it has locking pins (called a bayonet cap bulb), or by unscrewing it if it has a screw thread. Replace it with one of the same wattage. Many light fittings and lampshades have a label on them stating the maximum wattage you should use, and the fitting may overheat dangerously if you put in a higher wattage bulb just because you fancy a brighter room.
4. Replace the bulb. Keep your fingers well away from the light socket. Make sure to dispose of the old bulb safely, preferably by wrapping it so that it won't cut someone through a plastic bin liner.

When you go to buy a new bulb, take the old one with you, then you can't go wrong.

central light fittings require 100-watt ones. Wherever possible, replace regular light bulbs with energy saving ones. These are more expensive, but they use much less electricity than ordinary bulbs and last ten times longer.

● Fifth rule: do not overload sockets – either physically, by using lots of adaptors to take extra plugs, or electrically. Multiple adaptors overload the contacts inside the socket, causing sparking and possibly a fire. Each socket can supply up to 3000 watts (3 kilowatts) of power, so check the wattage marked on any appliance with a heating element (such as a kettle or a fan heater). These use a lot of power, so don't plug more than one into any socket or adaptor at the same time.

● And lastly, have a good torch available, and always keep it in the same place. If the lights have gone, it is very reassuring to have a torch handy and anyone who has experienced a power cut will know that it is essential. It is no good having a torch with no batteries, so check that it works now and again and keep a new set of spare batteries with it. Candles are good too and can be very comforting and romantic in a power cut, but a torch is more flexible, more transportable and a lot less dangerous. Besides, you can never find a match when you need one.

'The electricity went off in our house and none of us knew where to find the fuse box. We were in darkness for two hours until we found it. It was traumatic. Then we were terrified we might electrocute ourselves so we still had to go and get the boys from next door.' MATILDA, 20

'In college houses there are loads of adaptors into which you can stick about six plugs and all I know is that you have to be careful not to overload them.' HANNAH, 20

FIT FOR LIFE

WHEN YOU'RE AT SCHOOL YOU GET BLUDGEONED into playing games but you don't want to wait until you are fat and 40 to realise that you need to take an interest in your own fitness levels. The same goes for your cleansing routines. A bit of prevention can save a lot of anguish later.

In your teen years your body changes with puberty. The things you previously took for granted, such as clear skin and odour-free armpits can no longer be relied upon. it is time now to take control.

Check out your Body Mass Index rating. This is your height for weight ratio. Try *www.kidshealth.org* for a calculator for under-18s and if you are too high up the scale, put on your running shoes.

MINI QUIZ

Can you look after yourself without your mum or dad there to nag you?

1. How much water should you drink a day?
2. What factor sun cream should you use?
3. Can you name the best source of omega-3 fatty acids?
4. Which is the most important meal of the day?

Answers

1. At least 2 litres, or 8 glasses.
2. A minimum of Factor 15.
3. Oily fish.
4. Breakfast.

Dear Teenager,
17 HOW TO KEEP FIT AND HEALTHY

The statistics are alarming. Children today are often very unfit couch potatoes. A recent British report suggests that nine out of ten school children are not doing enough exercise to ensure that they grow up into healthy adults. That means that you are quite likely to be a couch potato, especially if you are a girl. Boys are more likely to kick a football around.

The consequences of this are massive. Obesity can lead to cardiovascular diseases and to diabetes. There are enough horrible illnesses out there for us all to get without inflicting more trouble on ourselves. You may hate sport. You may not like competitive games. You may not see yourself as the sporty type. But you should now make it your responsibility to keep fit and to have a healthy lifestyle.

Dieting is not the answer. It's not a question of Atkins versus high carb. It's a question of developing a sensible regime that involves eating well and exercising regularly. My top tips are:

- Always eat breakfast. All the studies show that kids who miss breakfast concentrate and perform less well at school.

- Make sure you eat at least five portions of fruit and vegetables a day. Only one of these can be a fruit juice.

- Drink lots of water. About 50–70 per cent of body weight is water. The recommended intake is 2 litres a day for an adult. You pee about 1.5 litres. You lose another litre breathing, sweating and in bowel movements. Food accounts for about 20 per cent of your water intake, so about 2 litres should replace the lost fluid. However, for some people this is barely enough and 5 litres may be optimal. If you don't have enough water, you suffer from dehydration, which makes you tired and stops your body functions from performing properly. Try carrying a bottle of water with you. Kids who drink enough water perform better at school.

- Try to avoid eating junk food. It's a very easy habit to start, but a difficult one to break. One typical fast food meal may contain more than 50 per cent of your daily fat allowance and almost 100 per cent of your daily saturated fat allowance. It's also likely to be high in salt and sugar. If you must have a take-away, limit yourself to one a week and pick the healthy option – see **How to Eat Healthier Take-Aways** for suggestions. Alternatively, have baked beans on wholemeal toast; a great snack which is cheap, filling and good for you.

● Take up some form of exercise, be it swimming, gym classes or a team sport. And if you really can't stomach the thought of that, make sure you do at least three x 30-minute walks a week. I know teenagers find it almost impossible to think about long-term consequences, but you are investing here for a lifetime. Your body, your life.

Dear Parents,

If you have children who won't touch a green vegetable, it is a worry. I've heard myself say, 'Oh, he won't touch broccoli,' numerous times. I now kick myself for not taking a firmer line when the children were very small, because I think these eating habits are set at a very young age and it becomes extremely hard to force-feed a 12 year old!

All the research suggests that the more children know about diet the more open they are to good food. I found that getting my children to count how many fruit and vegetables they had eaten that day to see if they made their five, was very helpful. They saw it as a personal goal to be reached. The experience of Jamie Oliver and his school dinners amply demonstrated that children's reluctance to try something new is very hard to overcome. It also showed that the consequences of poor diet (near permanent constipation and vomiting) are awful. I felt sufficiently worried about my children's diet at one time that I took stock, reviewed a week's menus and decided that some things had to change. I cut out puddings, introduced more pulses and gave very small portions of the food (I mean the vegetables!) that they didn't like. It also helped to say, 'Here are two vegetables. You can choose a serving of one or the other; you don't have to have both.' We're getting there slowly.

Dear Teenager,
18 HOW TO STAY CLEAN AND FRESH

When my (then) ten year old went away on a school trip for the first time, we packed him his toothbrush, soap, a flannel and a towel. I didn't have high hopes of the soap as he has barely ever come into close contact with it at home. But I was quite surprised when he came home after four days with a completely dry and clean towel. Asked if he'd washed at all, he just looked mystified and talked about something else.

I think girls often have more awareness of their skin and its needs, but for boys it can be an alien concept. Until the spots start to arrive. Prevention is better than cure and a decent skincare regime is a good habit for life. I know a 14-year-old girl who wouldn't come down for breakfast in the morning without being fully made up; and I know 14-year-old boys whose faces barely ever encounter even a flannel. Girls are much more conscious of and interested in skin care and skin products but the basics of looking after yourself and staying healthy are common to both sexes.

- Clean your skin well twice a day. I know it's boring but it's no good just poking some spot cream on the offending bit of face. There are millions of products on sale at the supermarket or chemist, but whatever you choose, just make a habit of cleaning thoroughly and regularly. My children clean their teeth every night but slop a flannel round their cheeks if they are feeling generous. You may get by like this aged seven. It won't work when your hormones are going haywire and you could land up a very spotty 17.

- If you wear make up, always take it off at night using a light cleanser and always using inward strokes around your eyes so as not to stretch the skin.

- Use a moisturiser. That includes boys. Boys' skin isn't fundamentally different and skin feels and looks better when it's not dried up.

● Teenagers are spotty. It just goes with the territory. With girls it can get even worse around your periods, which is grossly unfair. You will probably get blackheads, white heads and plain spots. The normal advice is, don't pick. You can make them worse by prodding and poking at them and even leave permanent scars. But the world is split into pickers and non-pickers and some people just find it irresistible.

● If you're unlucky enough to develop acne, you'll have a harder time. You can get over-the-counter treatments, usually benzoyl peroxide, which can be quite effective. Lots of people make the mistake of simply putting it on the spots. To get a reaction you need to put it all over your face. If that doesn't do the trick, find out as much information online as you can (there are lots of support groups) and go and see a doctor who can prescribe a stronger treatment. Be patient. It may take two to three months to sort out. The good news is that studies show that although acne causes stress, most kids with acne grow up remarkably well despite it.

● Clean and cut your nails. Don't chew them or you may be helping transfer threadworms and other nasties to your mouth.

● Look after your feet. With the thousands of steps you take each day, they suffer a lot from wear and tear, and nasty, cracking, dry skin can be painful. Use an aqueous cream (a special foot cream or E45) each night. Not only will your feet look and feel good, but the rest of you will too. Reflexologists will tell you that the well-being of your whole body rests in your feet, so don't ignore them.

● Don't rinse your hair in your bath water. You are just adding muck to it. Rinse it properly. Get your hair trimmed every couple of months or you will develop split ends.

● Drink masses of water. Always travel with a bottle and make sure you keep having sips throughout the day. If you are dehydrated, your skin will not look good. Your skin will look sad and you will look lethargic.

● Throw away the crisps and eat healthy snacks instead. Your skin will benefit.

● Get a decent night's sleep. Sleep deprivation shows very quickly in the skin, both with bags around the eyes and a lacklustre appearance.

● Relax. Take some time out to cool down and chill out. Go for a walk, meditate, take an exercise class or make yourself a fruit smoothie. Feel good and you'll look good.

 I know kids who can't sit still for a minute. Especially now, there are such pressures on them all the time: Do this, do that, buy this, buy that, have the right trainers. Then if they stop for a second they get bored. I meditate a lot. You need to be alone with yourself every now and again. Learn to enjoy your own company.

BENJAMIN ZEPHANIAH, POET AND NOVELIST

'There's one boy in our flat who only ever used to shower once a week. He's changed!' OLLIE, 18

'I have a girlfriend so I have to clean myself up when she comes round. I don't often wash my face and I don't ever wash my hair. It smells nicer when you don't wash it; more like hair and less like strawberries.' WILL, 18

www.skincarephysicians.com/acnenet (American Academy of Dermatology) offers lots of information about acne.

Dear Teenager,
19 HOW TO HAVE NICE SKIN, NOT SKIN CANCER

In Victorian times it was fashionable to be lily white. If you had a sun tan it was a sign that you were working outside. Now a tan has become a sign of flash holidays abroad and we associate tans with leisure and relaxation. We often feel better when we have got one, which is bad news because sun tans are actually a sign of skin damage. They are not healthy at all. Getting a tan can expose you to high risk of cancer. Most skin cancers are the result of ultra-violet radiation from over-exposure to the sun. Skin cancer is the most common form of cancer in the UK and the number of people who get it is increasing.

Ultra-violet radiation (UVR) penetrates the cells, causing sunburn, wrinkly skin, eye damage and cancer. You are most at risk if you have a fair skin or pale eyes. People with olive, brown or black skins have a lower risk.

The sun is not equally dangerous all the time. UVR is most dangerous when the sun's rays are most direct and intense, so summer is the highest risk season and midday, when the sun is at its highest point, is the riskiest time of day.

You can still be burnt by the sun on a cloudy day. We once spent a couple of hours on an overcast French beach. It was very disappointing weather. I am normally extremely careful about the children's exposure to the sun as they have very fair skin. However, that morning, because there was no sun, I said they could take their T-shirts off while they dug sandcastles. At lunchtime, I was amazed to find that one of the boys was badly burnt on his back. It turned out to be so serious that he had to be given treatment normally given to victims of fire. As a result of a few experiences like that I am much more careful now. We have invested in some UV filter T-shirts that block out the harmful rays and are good to wear when you are on the beach or swimming in the sea. Australians, who really know about the potentially damaging effects of the sun, often wear them.

- Sit in the shade. Don't cook in the sun.
- Always use sunscreen with a minimum of Factor 15 and one that says it is 'broad spectrum' (this protects against different rays). You don't need to go for an expensive brand.
- Apply sunscreen at least 15 minutes before you go into the sun. It does not work immediately.
- Check the sell-by date. Sunscreens last two to three years. I found some in my cupboard that were (ahhh!) over a decade old.
- Don't go out in the midday sun. That's only for mad dogs and Englishmen.
- Wear protective clothing, don't bare all. It's not worth it. Sunscreen does not offer complete protection.
- Reapply sunscreen every two hours and after going swimming.

SYMPTOMS OF SKIN CANCER

You need to be able to recognise the symptoms of skin cancer and if you spot any of them, you need to act immediately. As with most cancers, early detection makes it much more treatable.
There are two main sorts of skin cancer.

Malignant melanoma: This is the third most common type of cancer in 15–30 year olds. Look out for a new mole or an existing mole that gets larger or has a ragged outline or is a mixture of brown and black. Also look out for a mole that is enlarged, or oozes blood or crust. Basically, report any changes to moles to a doctor.

Non-melanoma: This is the most common type of skin cancer and may be lumps, spots, sores or ulcers or scaly patches, usually on the parts of the body most exposed to the sun. Check out anything unusual with your doctor. Fortunately it is usually easy to cure.

Knowledge about skin cancer is fairly recent. When I went on holiday as a child, we used to sunbathe all day. I look back and think, 'How could we have done that?' There is no excuse today. It is thought that many skin cancers are the result of skin damage during childhood.

If you were thinking that an indoor tan from a lamp or a sunbed would be OK, beware! According to Cancer Research UK, tanning lamps and sunbeds are not safe. They, too, are likely to increase your risk of skin cancer.

However, you're OK with getting a tan out of a bottle, though even that can be risky, but for different reasons. I once applied fake tan from a bottle but was completely inexpert at doing it. My face looked like a mask because there was a gap between the cream and my hairline. Also, I didn't wash my hands properly afterwards. My fingers stained deeply so that I was left looking like a smoker on 50 a day. Very attractive.

✳ **www.sunsmart.org.uk** offers information about staying safe in the sun. It also directs you to the Met office site where you can find the UV rating for the day, so you can measure the degree of risk.

Dear Teenager
20 HOW TO GET RID OF NITS

See if you can read this section without scratching your head...

People are often ashamed of nits and talk about them in hushed tones or, even worse, as something only other people get. In our house, we have competitions to see who has most of them. Top score has been about the 80 mark. Nits are most common among small children but I did once read in the paper that there was an outbreak of nits at the House of Commons and that all the honourable members were warned not to share hairbrushes. Most MPs don't look as if they comb their hair, let alone share their brushes.

Nits are the egg casings from lice. Lice are a few millimetres in length and have six legs. They can live for about 30 days and suck the blood from your scalp, yum, yum. They lay their eggs and glue them to your hair and after about seven days of this nice, warm environment, the eggs hatch and your nit score rockets.

Head lice walk from one head to another and you catch them by having your head close to someone else who is giving them head room. You can get them at any age but they are inevitably very common among primary school children. Lice prefer clean, non-greasy hair, so having them is not a sign of bad hygiene. The commonest sign of lice is an itchy scalp. You may also be able to see the little white nits (smaller than a pin head), which can be mistaken for dandruff.

There are thousands of nit treatments at the chemists and on the internet, but, frankly, they are not always worth the bother. Usually all you need is a nit comb (which is a comb with very fine teeth) and a bottle of conditioner.

● Wash your hair as normal. Add the conditioner.

● Run the comb through your hair very carefully and you'll find the nits stuck to the comb. This is when you start counting. In my experience, they like hiding behind the ears and at the base of the neck.

● Wipe the nits from the comb onto a paper towel. When you have evicted them all, rinse out the conditioner.

● You need to use the nit comb every three days for a fortnight. You'll get rid of them easily, and they'll probably be back just as easily. They may be uninvited guests on your head, but, honestly, there are so many worse things than can happen, they are just not worth making a fuss about.

'I have long hair and I've had nits twice. I would use every possible medication, well beyond what is needed. And a nit comb. I'd blast them and kill every one.' ALEXIS, 18

'I haven't had nits in years but I quite like them. It's something to do. It's quite rewarding to get one on a comb.' WILL, 18

www.nhsdirect.nhs.uk has helpful advice on how to deal with nits. Use the search function to find the head lice page.

Dear Teenager,
21 HOW TO HAVE A BALANCED DIET

I don't think I ever thought very much about what I was eating until I had children and started to put on weight. In some respects I think that's fine: we shouldn't spend time worrying about weight, especially when we're young. In recent years we have all become diet obsessed and books, newspapers, magazines and TV shows all sell on the basis of gimmicky new diets, which will help you lose kilos/pounds/stones in days/weeks/months. We seem to want to believe their promises and set off to starve ourselves or eat only cabbage, or oranges and peanuts, or no carbs, or low carbs or diet drinks or pills. It's all daft because ultimately we all know that what we need is simply a balanced diet and plenty of exercise.

> ## THE MAIN FOOD GROUPS
> *You should make sure that you are eating food from each of the following four food groups every day.*
>
> ● **Cereals:** bread, potatoes, rice, breakfast cereal, pasta.
>
> ● **Fruit and vegetables:** remember your five fruit and vegetables each day. Apparently most adults only manage to eat three.
>
> ● **Milk and dairy:** milk, cheese or yogurt.
>
> ● **Proteins:** meat, fish, eggs, nuts and pulses.

However, in the time between my childhood and that of my children, we have become much more dependent on processed foods. Often we have little idea what is in them and even more often we wouldn't like it if we knew. More and more kids are growing up not knowing how to cook for themselves and that processed food dependency will just carry on increasing. That means we all need to know more about what makes a healthy diet and to make sure one way or another that we get it.

Obesity is a big, fat problem today. So is heart disease. This section contains some basic food rules and some suggestions for getting into good habits.

● **Dieting:** Try not to diet. If you insist on doing it, expect to lose 1 or 2 pounds (between ½ and 1 kilogram) a week. A pound (about ½ a kilogram) of fat contains 3,500 calories so to lose a pound (½ a kilogram) a week, you need to cut out 500 calories a day (or take more exercise to burn them up). Drink semi-skinned milk. Cut down on the amount of sugar you consume but don't do a mad diet and try to lose lots of weight very quickly. You'll only put it back on again. All that effort for nothing!

● **Snacking:** Snacking is not a bad thing. It depends what you snack on. Try nuts or dried fruits or chopped carrots or rice crackers. Or, if you have a liquidiser, make a fruit smoothie. Forget the crisps. They are bad news.

- **Water:** Drink lots of it. If your urine is dark in colour, instead of pale, you're not drinking enough. Aim for 8 glasses a day.

- **Eat breakfast:** Up to a third of us miss breakfast and yet people who eat breakfast are thought to have more balanced diets than those who miss the first meal of the day. I am passionate about porridge to get the day off to a good start. It gives you slow release energy and stops you being hungry until lunch.

- **Eat 5 portions of fruit and veg a day:** The more fruit and veg you eat the better and five portions should be your minimum. Fruit and veg are packed with vitamins, minerals and fibre. Frozen and canned foods count; potatoes don't. What counts as a portion? One apple or banana; two small fruit such as satsumas or kiwi; seven strawberries or 14 cherries; two broccoli spears; three heaped tablespoons of carrots or peas.

- **Eat less salt:** The average adult salt intake in the West is 9.5 grams a day (which is about 2 teaspoons). It is supposed to be 6 grams. Three-quarters of the salt we eat is already added to the food we buy and processed food often contains a lot. Read how much salt or sodium is listed in the ingredients (see **How to Understand Food Labels** to convert the measures).

- **Avoid saturated fat:** The body needs fat but not too much, and not the wrong kind. Try to avoid fry-ups. Saturated fats also include animal fats in meat and poultry; dairy products; processed and fast foods. Unsaturated fat, which your body does need, is found in avocado pears, vegetable oils and fish.

- **Eat fish:** Fish can be hard to get used to eating if you're not in the habit but the government recommendation is for two portions of fish a week, one of them oily (like sardines).

Most of us in the developed world are lucky enough to have good food available to us. Take pleasure in the food you eat. Eat with friends when you can. Eat slowly. Savour each and every mouthful.

'By the time I was 12 I could cook a meal. I know how to do a healthy, balanced meal too. I'm proud of that!' KACHENGA, 19

'I eat a lot of fruit and vegetables. Without fail I eat an apple a day, it's just habit. I'm not health mad at all and I'd hate to watch what I eat. You just have to eat fruit and veg, and take some exercise. I walk to work each day, which is about 3 ½ miles. When I see the utterly stupid diets of some of the people I work for and the way they drink Diet Coke as if it were water, I despair!' TOM, 19

 www.bda.uk.com (British Dietetic Association) offers information about everything from having healthy snacks to a healthy heart.

Dear Parents,

Life is complicated enough without being blamed for our children's obesity problems. However, eating habits are established young. I really wish now that I had fed my babies on carrot sticks and broccoli spears from the first moment they could chew. Instead I have one who hates anything green, one who hates tomatoes and one who eats like a horse.

When they were still quite little, my mum suggested giving them a picnic each evening. The picnic is actually a bowl of chopped up fruit, usually an apple, pear and banana each. It soon became a matter of habit and now none of the three of them can finish the evening without their picnic. I suspect they will now go on through life eating fruit each evening. It's an easy way of building towards their five fruits and veg a day. When friends come to stay the night they sometimes think it's weird but my kids think it's weird when they go to other people's houses and don't get given a picnic!

Dear Teenager,
22 HOW TO FEED YOUR BRAIN

It's all very well having a healthy body but you need a healthy brain too and some research is suggesting that your brain, like the rest of you, reaps rewards from your feeding it well. Tests done on school children apparently show that their learning and their behaviour are significantly affected by feeding them well and in particular by feeding them fish oils. Feed them on junk food and you'll have a class full of maniacs. Feed them sardines or fish supplements and you might have a class of well-behaved Einsteins. The same goes for you. If you want to improve your capacity to concentrate and turn your brain into a top-performing organ, then try feeding it right.

So what does your brain like to eat?

- Apparently it likes to eat breakfast. We all perform mental tasks better after a proper breakfast. Milk and cereals are good. So is toast. That's a performance enhancer and if you throw a few baked beans on top and a lashing of marmite, your brain (say the researchers) will be raring to go. Marmite's got good B vitamins but beans on toast will make you cleverer! According to one study, baked beans, which are rich in fibre, improve your cognition.

- Moving on to your lunch and tea, your brain requires omega-3 essential fats to function well. Research in this area is only in its infancy but some studies suggest children may read better, spell better and behave better if they eat these fats. You should be able to give yourself a couple of servings a week, but if you can't, you can buy fish oils as a vitamin supplement. See page 72 for a list of food sources.

- Your brain also relishes regular servings of fresh fruit and vegetables. When your gran said, 'Eat your greens,' she was probably trying to make you brainy. Fruit and veg are a rich source of antioxidants, which the brain requires to attack free radicals, the molecules that impair your memory. You can find antioxidants in strawberries, raspberries, red grapes, cherries, spinach and broccoli.

- Top of the list of antioxidants is the cranberry. I'm sure when I was young I never met a cranberry outside a muffin. Now the supermarkets are packed with them. According to research, the humble cranberry is so powerful that it can reduce brain impairment after strokes. Concentrate equivalent to half a cup of

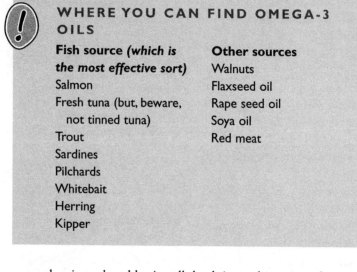

WHERE YOU CAN FIND OMEGA-3 OILS

Fish source *(which is the most effective sort)*
Salmon
Fresh tuna (but, beware, not tinned tuna)
Trout
Sardines
Pilchards
Whitebait
Herring
Kipper

Other sources
Walnuts
Flaxseed oil
Rape seed oil
Soya oil
Red meat

cranberries reduced brain cell death in stroke patients by 50 per cent. No wonder cranberries are marketed in some supermarkets now as Revision Food. Eat cranberries and become an A* pupil!

Well, that's what some researchers say. But the research is quite new and sceptics argue that it needs to be taken with a pinch of academic salt. But even if you think the case for brain food still has a way to go before it is proven, don't forget that your brain, like the rest of you, definitely requires regular exercise, lots of water and plenty of sleep. I can't promise you'll get top grades in every subject, but at least you'll have a fighting chance.

Dear Teenager,
23 HOW TO HAVE THE RIGHT IMMUNISATIONS

Everyone knows someone at school who fainted when the nurse gave them an injection. It's all part of the school ritual. Beyond that, most of us don't think very often about immunisations until we plan to travel somewhere exotic on holiday and suddenly find we need to know whether we're up to date on our jabs.

The national immunisation programme has helped to eradicate several dangerous diseases. It used to be commonplace for children to die of diphtheria for example, but now the disease has largely disappeared in the UK.

Regular immunisations

Babies today receive 10 jabs by the time they are 13 months old. Before they reach school age, children are protected against diphtheria, tetanus, whooping cough, polio, Hib, Meningitis C, pneumococcal meningitis, mumps, measles and rubella. Between the ages of 13 and 18 teenagers routinely get top-up protection against tetanus, diphtheria and polio.

If you are going away to study, most colleges want to know whether you are up to date with your immunisation programme. You need to keep a record of the dates and jabs you have had. If you have lost it, your GP surgery should be able to supply you with one.

Travel immunisations

If you are going travelling to some far-flung destination, you need to check your immunisation requirements in good time. Read up in guide books, or check with your GP or a specialist travel clinic what's required for your particular destination. This is best done at least eight weeks before departure. Courses of travel vaccines (if you are up to date on all the standard ones listed above) are usually given over a four-week period. Some vaccinations require more than one shot over a period of a few weeks. For some, such as yellow fever, you need a certificate that only becomes valid ten days after the jab has been given. Allow plenty of time.

Make sure to take the correct precautions regarding malaria. You can catch malaria from mosquito bites and it is a very unpleasant and potentially fatal illness. You can't be immunised against it but you can take a course of anti-malarial drugs. These sometimes need to be taken weeks before departure and continued for several weeks after.

Some GP surgeries offer travel advice but no immunisations. Others offer the full range of immunisations. Some charge and some offer jabs for free. There is one jab you always have to pay for and that is yellow fever. It can cost anything from £30 to £50.

You can also go to centres such as Trailfinders or British Airways Travel Clinics. You will have to pay for everything here.

'You don't think when you go to university that you'll need all these jabs. It's quite surprising. Luckily I'd pretty much had them all except for meningitis and flu.' JOCASTA, 18

www.nhsdirect.nhs.uk for information on the whys, whens and wherefores of all jabs including travel ones.

FIRST-AID BOX

MOST OF US WANT OUR MUM when we're feeling unwell but she's not always going to be available. If you are ever in doubt, call a doctor or NHS Direct (or 999 if it is an emergency) but often there are a few simple actions you can take to help yourself feel better. Usually it's not rocket science. It can come down to a good sleep and drinking lots of water.

It's also sensible to arm yourself with a bit of practical know-how to help other people in an emergency. You've seen *ER*. Learn how to do some life-saving manoeuvres yourself. But don't just rely on your telly-watching. Get properly trained.

Here are some pointers about when to tuck yourself up under the duvet and when to call for medical help.

MINI QUIZ

Are you a hypochondriac or a new recruit for the staff of ER?

1. How do you treat a virus?
2. How do you do the Tumbler Test for septicaemia?
3. Can you demonstrate the recovery position?
4. At what age can you give blood?

Answers

1. No, you don't treat it with antibiotics. You take a paracetamol and go to bed.
2. Press the glass against a skin rash to see if it fades. If it doesn't, call 999.
3. Lie on the floor and try it. Everyone should know how to do it.
4. 17 until 70.

Dear Teenager,

24 HOW TO KNOW THE DIFFERENCE BETWEEN A BACTERIUM AND A VIRUS

When people feel really sick they usually want lots of sympathy and looking after, as well as some medicine from the doctor to make them better. Patients are then sometimes disappointed when they leave the doctor's surgery without a prescription. They feel they are not being taken seriously. It's not that. It's a misunderstanding about the difference between viruses and bacteria.

Viruses and bacteria are the two commonest types of microbes or bugs to make us sick but they are as different from one another as chalk and cheese. They don't look alike, they are not the same size and they reproduce entirely differently. Bacteria are single-cell organisms that contain all they need to reproduce. Viruses attack other cells and they inject their genes into them or are eaten by them. They cannot reproduce on their own.

If you have a viral infection, there is no point in having antibiotics. They will not do the trick. A common viral infection will be cured by rest, drinking lots of water and time. You can also help to stop the spread of the infection by washing your hands before going near food. Some viral infections come from uncooked meat or raw eggs so you should also make sure that food is prepared correctly.

If you have a bacterial infection, then you will require antibiotics, which will kill off the guilty microbes. Sir Alexander Fleming discovered the first antibiotic, penicillin, in the late 1920s and they have been fantastically useful ever since. When you are prescribed antibiotics, you must finish the course of treatment (even if you feel better before the end) and take them exactly as it says on the label. Otherwise the bacteria infecting you may develop a resistance to antibiotics.

There is an increasing problem today of antibiotic resistance with hospital superbugs killing a few thousand people each year. This has happened because antibiotics have been over-prescribed down the years, both for animals and for humans. If you develop resistance to one antibiotic drug, you may have to move on to another, but the resistant bacteria may proliferate and become harder to fight.

So when you next feel ill, don't demand a spoonful of medicine from your GP if he or she says you don't need it. A painkiller to soothe you and to take your temperature down and a good bit of

BUG ATTACKS

Viral infections
Colds and flu
Most sore throats
Most coughs
Measles, German measles
Mumps
Chicken pox
Often several parts of the body affected

Bacterial infections
Some sore throats
Urinary tract infections
Most ear and sinus infections
Often a single part of the body affected

bed rest will really help. However, if you're still ill and worried, go back to your GP. Sometimes doctors simply don't know if an infection is from a virus or bacteria. In the olden days they may well have erred on the side of caution and given you antibiotics just in case. These days they go the other way and may be reluctant to give antibiotics. You may have an infection from bacteria after all. In my experience, other people's ear and throat infections are viral. Mine require antibiotics. But then life is full of inequalities. The men in my house get flu when I only get the common cold.

 www.nhsdirect.nhs.uk for further advice if you think you are suffering from a bacterium or a virus.

Dear Teenager,
25 HOW TO SPOT THE SIGNS OF MENINGITIS AND SEPTICAEMIA

Meningitis is the inflammation of the lining around the brain and spinal cord. It can be caused by different organisms including bacteria and viruses. Some bacteria that cause meningitis can also cause septicaemia (blood poisoning). Viral meningitis is a more common form of meningitis and is not usually serious. Bacterial meningitis and septicaemia can be very serious indeed. People who receive prompt diagnosis and treatment can recover fully. However if you do not recognise the symptoms you may not act fast enough. It can kill within hours, so time is of the essence.

Most people nowadays are vaccinated against meningitis C as a baby. This is an effective vaccine against one form of meningitis. It will not protect you against other strains including meningitis B, the most common form of bacterial meningitis. From 2006, babies will also be vaccinated against pneumococcal meningitis.

The symptoms are not the same and not everyone experiences all the symptoms. That's why you need to know the possibilities and not mistake the symptoms for a hangover or the flu.

Many people associate meningitis with a stiff neck and a dislike of bright lights. It is important to know that these are not symptoms of septicaemia. Septicaemia can occur with or without meningitis. Don't agonise about whether you might be mistaken because the patient doesn't have a stiff neck. Get medical help straight away. You could be saving a life.

There is a test you can try if you think someone may have septicaemia (see box opposite).

SPOTTING THE SYMPTOMS

Symptoms of meningitis
Severe headache
Stiff neck
Dislike of bright lights
Fever/vomiting
Drowsiness

Symptoms of septicaemia
A rash on the body that doesn't fade under pressure
Fever/vomiting
Cold hands and feet and/or shivering
Rapid breathing
Stomach, joint or muscle pain
Drowsiness

> ! If you see a rash on someone's skin, anywhere from head to toes, do the Tumbler Test. Press a glass against a septicaemic rash and the marks will not fade. You will still be able to see the marks through the glass. If this happens, call 999 for an ambulance at once.

 www.meningitis.trust.org is the site of the Meningitis Trust. It has a 24-hour nurse-led helpline.

Dear Teenager,

26 HOW TO KNOW IF YOU ARE ILL

My children always ask me to assess their degree of illness and when I'm sick I usually ask my mum. When you're feeling rough and you have a sore throat and your head hurts, you're not always in the best state to know whether you should take to your bed, ring the doctor or rush to the hospital. The decision is too much on top of everything else you are suffering.

If there is an emergency, clearly you must call 999. (Check the **How to Call Emergency Services** section for details.) If you want to wait to go and see your GP because you think you need treatment, that's fine. Otherwise, you can call NHS Direct, which is a 24-hour phone service staffed by nurses and professional advisers.

I've called this service on several occasions and found it really useful. Once, it resulted in the nurse phoning a doctor and arranging a house call within the hour. On another occasion I was told to give a child a different over-the-counter medicine and to call my GP in the morning if the problem persisted. It didn't. The medicine did the trick. It is very reassuring to talk to someone and to be able to run through all the symptoms. I think this is particularly useful if you are living away from home with no mum to turn to. The service won't leave you in agony to die of your symptoms after refusing to take them seriously. But they may either tell you to call 999 now or allow you to go to bed and get a good night's sleep feeling happier.

NHS Direct also have a website, which, as well as being a hypochondriac's haven with everything from abscesses to autism and warts to wisdom teeth, is an excellent guide to common illnesses and treatments. You can also find other health information on it, such as where to find the nearest open pharmacy or how to find an NHS walk-in surgery.

Not feeling well?

Colds and flu: If you have a runny nose, or are a bit sweaty, or you're sneezing or coughing and have general aches and pains, take a couple of paracetamol and go to bed. A glass of hot water with lemon juice squeezed in and a dollop of honey helps a lot. Keep drinking lots of water. Colds and flu cannot be treated with antibiotics.

Sore throats: Sore throats are often viral and are treated the same way as colds and flu. Try sucking some echinacea sweets for relief. But if your throat or glands are swollen or the condition persists, see a doctor. You might have tonsillitis, which is treatable with antibiotics.

Diarrhoea: If it is severe or painful or there is blood in your stools, see a doctor. Otherwise, avoid milk and other dairy products for a day and drink lots of (non-alcoholic) liquids. Diarrhoea can make the oral contraceptive less effective.

Period pains: If I knew the answer to this one I would be very rich. Between 40 and 70 per cent of women suffer and the ones who suffer most are the youngest. You can try paracetamol and some physical exercise. You can try non-steroidal anti-inflammatory drugs (NSAIDs), which you can buy over the counter. Stronger painkillers are available from the doctor.

 www.nhsdirect.nhs.uk (Tel: 0845 4647) can be called day or night for health advice. There are separate phone numbers for Scotland, Northern Ireland and Wales, which are given on the website.

Dear Teenager
27 HOW TO SIGN UP WITH A DOCTOR, DENTIST AND OPTICIAN

Dentists

I used to be a dental nurse so I can say with good authority that you should find yourself a dentist. This is easier said than done since there is a profound shortage of NHS dentists. In some areas the shortage is so acute that when an announcement is made that a new one is opening, people queue around the block to register. If you are moving away to college, you may automatically be offered a dentist. If not, or if you are moving off on your own, check with NHS Direct for dentists in your area. When you get a dentist, check how often you need to visit in order not to be taken off their register.

Research shows that people who go to the dentist regularly have fewer problems than people who only go in a crisis. If you are lucky and you were taken to the dentist every six months as a child, you probably won't be terrified of going and probably have good teeth. Don't let those good habits lapse when you leave home. (The current recommendation is to go to the dentist according to clinical need at intervals of between 3 and 24 months.) You want your teeth to last a lifetime so you need to look after them. If you haven't been regularly, start now. It's free until you are 18 (or 19 in full-time education) and better to endure the fear of the dentist's chair now than look forward to 50 years with false teeth.

NHS treatments are as good as private ones. The difference is, not every treatment is available on the NHS. You can't get white fillings on the NHS so you might want to pay for one if you've got decay in a tooth that is visible. You will be charged the private rate. It is also worth paying to have your teeth cleaned by a hygienist at least once a year. It feels as if someone is treating your mouth as a quarry, but the results are brilliant. It's very helpful in keeping your gums healthy, and if your gums are healthy your teeth are less likely to fall out. Your mouth needs to be especially clean if you are wearing a brace. It feels to me as if every 15 year old wears a brace. Along with charity wristbands, they are a key fashion accessory.

Given the shortage of dentists, and given that it's a fairly lucrative profession, perhaps you should consider it as a career choice.

PAYING FOR PRESCRIPTIONS

● Students up to the age of 19 are exempt from prescription charges and eye test charges.
● After that, it's a standard cost for every prescribed item.
● A dental check-up and scale and polish will set you back about £15 but you will have to pay more for X-rays and treatment.
● Contraceptives are free from surgeries and clinics.

Doctors

Doctors are easier to find than dentists. However doctors will not take you if their list is full and you may need to shop around. The local primary care trust or NHS Direct will help you find one. You should make sure you are always registered with a GP. Do not wait until you are sick. If you are going away to college, it is not uncommon for a mixture of everybody's germs, known as freshers' flu, to strike early in term. Register with a local doctor (some colleges have their own health centres) before you get it. Best of all is a doctor within walking distance. It's much easier when you have the squits or you are coughing your guts out to make it to the surgery on the corner than to contemplate getting on a bus or cadging a lift.

You can get contraception from your GP or you can choose to go to a family planning clinic. If you are living away from home in term time, you can continue to go to see your doctor at home as a temporary patient.

Opticians

You are entitled to free eye check-ups (and a voucher towards the cost of glasses) up to the age of 16, or 19 if you are still in full-time education. All you have to do is bowl along to a high street shop to book an appointment with an optometrist. These are the people qualified to give eye examinations whereas opticians fit and sell glasses.

If you wear glasses, you need to go for annual check-ups in case you need a new prescription. If you don't wear glasses, there's no real need to go. Naturally if you have any trouble with your vision you should seek help right away. Most changes in vision happen between babyhood and the age of 7 and at around 12. After that, according to my optician, you're likely to be all right until you're 40. It's downhill after that.

www.nhsdirect.nhs.uk will tell you how to find a doctor or a dentist in your area.

Dear Teenager,
28 HOW TO GIVE BLOOD

If you're in an accident or you need an operation you may well find that you need a blood transfusion. It could save your life. For that to happen there needs to be a supply of blood in the blood bank, but the blood also needs to be a correct match. Indeed, if you are given the wrong type it could be the death of you.

You can be one of several different blood groups. You can also be negative or positive. Someone who is A- cannot be given the blood of someone who is A+. This means that the National Blood Service, the keepers of most of the nation's blood supply, needs regular donations of blood from donors of all blood types. In fact every year they take 2.5 million donations of just under a pint each.

You can help top up the nation's blood supply as soon as you are 17. You can find out your nearest centre by looking up the National Blood Service on the internet at *www.blood.co.uk*.

The procedure isn't scary. You need to make sure you eat and drink before you go. You will be asked to complete a questionnaire. Then a tiny drop of blood will be taken from your finger. It's just a pin prick to check your haemoglobin levels to make sure that you are not anaemic. About 470 ml (just under a pint) of blood is then taken from your arm. The body has about 5 litres of blood and makes up for the lost blood very quickly. You will rest for a couple of

Q. *What percentage of the eligible population in the UK gives blood?*
A. 6%

WHO CAN GIVE BLOOD?

You must be between 17 and 60 (although regular donors can go on to the age of 70).

You must weigh more than 50 kg.

You must not have given blood within the last 16 weeks.

You must not be suffering from a cold, a sore throat or a cough.

You must not be pregnant or have a small baby.

You must not be on antibiotics.

You must not have suffered from jaundice or hepatitis within 12 months, or have HIV.

You must not be undergoing hospital tests or waiting for surgery.

You must not have had body piercing or tattooing, semi-permanent make-up or acupuncture in the last 6 months. (There is an exception made for NHS certificated acupuncture.)

You must say if you are on any medication.

You must not have had a blood transfusion in the UK since 1980 (this is protection against the spread of variant Creutzfeldt-Jakob disease).

You must not ever have injected yourself with a drug.

You may not donate if you are a man who has had sex with another man (even safe sex).

minutes and then be rewarded by a drink and biscuits and a strong sense of having done a good thing. The whole procedure takes less than an hour. Your blood will undergo lots of checks to determine what type it is and that it is safe to give to a patient.

Once you have given blood, you will know it is easy and you'll want to do it again. The National Blood Service encourages donors to give three times a year and it has rewards for long service. Once you pass big milestones (50 donations upwards) you get presents of gold pins and brooches, crystal tumblers and decanters. I'm not sure they are much of a draw but it's nice for those regular donors to know that they are appreciated.

Unfortunately, you can go straight back to school, university or work after giving blood...

'My friends and I tend to go and do it together and then go out afterwards for a meaty meal to make up the blood! And you're not meant to drink afterwards but you do get drunk more quickly and cheaply after giving blood I find.' MATILDA, 20

'I've just had a piercing so I'm not allowed to at the moment, but I will.'
HANNAH, 20

www.blood.co.uk (Tel: 0845 7 711 711) is the National Blood Service. Phone or use the internet site to find out where and how to give blood.

Dear Teenager,
29 HOW TO DONATE YOUR ORGANS

Sometimes a living person will donate an organ to a friend or family member. This is most common with the kidney. You've got two of them but you only need one. However, most transplants take place after someone has been in an accident such as a car crash and has died in hospital. Out of the tragedy of one person's untimely death, someone else can be given the gift of life.

Organs that can be transplanted include the heart, lungs, kidney, pancreas, liver and small bowel. In addition, tissue, including the corneas, skin, bone and heart valves can be transplanted.

Three thousand transplants happen in the UK each year but 6,000 people are waiting for an organ. In 2004, 400 people died while waiting for a transplant.

Twelve million people in Britain have offered to be donors in the event of their death. Some people like to carry a donor card, which gives details of their next of kin, but the best thing to do is to put yourself on the NHS Organ Donor Register. When someone dies in hospital, the register is immediately checked to see if they were willing to donate organs.

The other important thing to do is to talk to your family about your wishes. A transplant will only be carried out with the consent of the next of kin, even if you are on the donor register, so you should let your parents or family know that this is your intention. Otherwise they may say no.

There is no minimum age either for organ donation or for registering. It's horrid to think about anyone dying but helping someone else to live is so important, and the anguish that people go through waiting and hoping for an organ is so great that it has to be thought about. God forbid that any of my family dies, but if they did I would be happy to know that they had helped someone else to live.

'I don't carry a card but my parents know that I want to give my organs if anything happened to me. I must sign up.' HANNAH, 20

❋ **www.uktransplant.org.uk (Tel: 0845 60 60 400)** to sign up to be a donor.

Dear Teenager,
30 HOW TO SAVE A LIFE

We should all know how to do basic first aid. When something goes wrong it is terrifying and if you have been trained in first aid it's likely that the training will kick in automatically and you can save a life, rather than standing around panicking, wishing you knew what on earth to do.

The best thing is to sign up for a short course, even a couple of hours, so that you get to try out the techniques. As well as the basics here, ideally you should learn when to move or not to move someone and how to cope with babies and children as well as adults. St John Ambulance offer first-aid courses up and down the country.

Check for danger

The first thing to do at an incident is to make sure that you and the casualty are not in danger. When I stopped to help a man who had been thrown off his bike into the middle of the road, I was so panicked by his state that I forgot to look at the mayhem all around us. A much wiser person started to re-direct the traffic. If you are helping a casualty, ask someone to do this for you and to ring the emergency services.

Recovery position (adults)

If the casualty is breathing (place your cheek next to their nose and mouth to feel or hear their breath), put them in the recovery position. This means turning the casualty on their side with their uppermost arm outstretched towards you to support their upper body and their uppermost leg bent at the knee to support their lower body.

Rescue breaths or kiss of life (adults)

If the casualty is not breathing, tilt their head back so that their chin is sticking up. This is to free their airways. Place your mouth firmly over theirs and blow. Give a full breath until his or her chest rises. Remove your mouth, let the chest fall and repeat the procedure. Check the casualty's pulse by placing your fingers on the side of their neck. If you cannot feel a pulse, start chest compressions.

Chest compressions (adults)

Place one hand on the centre of the casualty's chest just below their nipples. Place your other hand on top and press down with your palm. Depress the chest by about 4 centimetres. Repeat. After 15 compressions, give 2 rescue breaths and repeat this sequence until help arrives. Chest compressions need to be done at a speed of about 100 a minute.

Heimlich Manoeuvre

If an adult is choking, stand behind the casualty and wrap your arms around their waist. Form one hand into a fist and point the thumb below the breast bone into the victim's stomach. Put your other hand on top and thrust inwards and upwards several times. This should

WHO WAS HEIMLICH?

The Heimlich Manoeuvre was designed in 1974 by Dr Heimlich, who was finally called upon to use his own technique for the first time in 2000 at the grand old age of 83 on a fellow diner in a restaurant. Choking is very common and the Heimlich Manoeuvre is said to have saved the lives of hundreds of thousands of people, including President Ronald Reagan and actress Elizabeth Taylor.

eject the foreign object. If it doesn't, repeat the procedure two or three times. If the obstruction still does not clear, dial 999 for an ambulance. If you are choking, and you're on your own, you can perform the procedure on yourself. Equally, you can lean over a table or chair back and press your stomach forcefully against the edge to try to pop out the object.

These instructions tell you some of the basics but the only way to feel confident in an emergency is to have had some practice. The techniques you need to use on adults are often different from those you need for children or babies. Have a go at putting someone in the recovery position to prove you can do it. And then invest in that first-aid course and learn the techniques from a qualified instructor. It might save a life.

'If someone collapsed in front of me I think I'd call 999 and hope that the person at the other end would tell me what to do.' TIAN, 20

'I trained as a lifeguard and work at the swimming pool so I had to learn how to do this. I wouldn't have known otherwise.' IAN, 19

www.sja.org.uk (St John Ambulance) will give you more detailed first-aid advice as well as details of first-aid courses available near you.

Dear Teenager,
31 HOW TO DEAL WITH BLEEDING AND BURNS

Bleeding
Some people can't stand the sight of blood. My son Ben goes all faint if he pricks his finger, and I'm not very faint-proof myself. However, if something serious happens, you need to be able to drop into automatic mode and know what to do.

If you are dealing with a minor cut, wash your hands and put on a pair of sterile gloves to protect yourself. Clean the cut under running water. Pat it dry with a sterile dressing and, if it's possible, hold it above the patient's heart.

If the cut is more serious, call 999 for an ambulance. Lie the casualty down. Apply a clean cloth to the wound until a sterile dressing is available. Direct pressure is good for external bleeding. Apply a bandage to the sterile dressing, tightly enough to help control the bleeding but not so tightly that it stops circulation. If an object such as a knife is in the wound, do not remove it. Place bandages around the object.

You may be feeling in a panic yourself but you also have to give the patient reassurance and comfort, so try to stay calm.

Burns

Most people know that if you have a small burn you should cover it in running water, but most people don't know that that doesn't mean just shoving your finger under the tap for a few seconds. The burn should be held under running water for at least ten minutes. If you later develop blisters, don't pop them.

If the burn is more extensive, call 999 for an ambulance. If you can, remove any jewellery from the affected area unless it is sticking to the skin (wear disposable gloves to do this).

Cover the burn with something that is not fluffy. A clean plastic bag or kitchen cling-film are both good options.

Remember the casualty is likely to be in shock and will need to be kept warm and given reassurance.

Lots of burns are caused by people getting into scalding hot baths. Always test the temperature of the bath with your hand first. Other common causes of burns are hot drinks, saucepans of hot liquids and boiling kettles.

'I did two first-aid courses at school so I know what to do. Also I learnt from my mum. When I burnt my arm, she put it under cold water for ten minutes, then wrapped it in cling-film. You take it for granted that your mum knows what to do, and some of it then rubs off.'
KACHENGA, 19

 www.sja.org.uk (St John Ambulance) for more information on treating bleeding and burns.

Dear Teenager,
32 HOW TO BE PREPARED FOR AN ACCIDENT

It is part of the human condition to think that accidents always happen to other people but if there is an emergency in your house, it is as well to be equipped for it.

● **Have a first-aid kit:** Everyone should have one. You can make your own, if you feel inclined, or you can simply buy one. It should contain: sterile gauzes, bandages, antiseptic wipes, scissors, safety pins, plastic gloves and antiseptic cream. It is also a good idea to have a thermometer for when you want to prove how ill you are and a packet of ibuprofen tablets for aches and pains. I always keep Micropore tape in mine because it is easy to use and nicer than regular plasters. The trick with first-aid kits is to replenish them as you use them.

● **Test your smoke alarm:** Every house should have one on every floor. Make sure yours is working. Fire-fighters despair of people who think their job is done when they have an alarm fitted but then never test the batteries. If there is a fire, a fire alarm will only help you if it's operating.

● **Have a fire blanket:** Have a fire blanket in the kitchen in case you have a stove fire. If you are renting a house, the landlord is obliged to provide one.

● **Test the gas and the electrics:** Again, in rented accommodation, the landlord has to have any gas appliance checked by a CORGI-registered practitioner annually. He or she is also responsible for the safety of any electrical appliances. It is your responsibility as tenant to provide him or her with access. Make sure that the tests are up to date.

● **Do a first-aid course:** Sign up for a first-aid course so you would know what to do in an emergency.

SAFETY FIRST

ONE OF PARENTS' BIGGEST WORRIES is about whether their children will be safe when they fly the nest. We spend so many years shepherding you across roads and collecting you from late night parties that it is hard to let you go without some sense of alarm. You will go out into the big, bad world and the best we can do is to equip you to cope with it.

This chapter deals with troubles that none of us want, such as being mugged or having a drink spiked. It includes other potential ills we choose for ourselves, such as tattoos and piercings. What these things all have in common is the need for you to take the right precautions.

'I've always been paranoid about security and we were always hearing stories of awful things happening. One boy in our house was hopeless. He did ridiculous things. He left the front door open. He left his bedroom window open, which was on the ground floor. And he nearly set the house on fire. I was happy to move back into college to have my own space.' ANNA, 24

MINI QUIZ

Are you as safe as houses or an accident waiting to happen?

1. What precaution can you take to avoid your drink being spiked?
2. What percentage of street crime involves mobiles?
3. When is it appropriate to call 999?

Answers

1. Never leave your drink unattended.
2. 50%.
3. If you are in immediate danger or a crime is happening now – the perpetrators may still be in the area.

Dear Teenager,
33 HOW TO NOT BE MUGGED

Actually, it's not possible to tell you this. Being mugged is awful and you can't always stop it happening by acting differently. It's not your fault; it's not something you bring upon yourself. Street crime is a huge and growing problem and teenagers, especially boys, are vulnerable to it.

One of the main culprits is the mobile phone. They are valuable, they are easy to pinch and the muggers know that lots of young teens carry them. It is 'easy pickings'.

Unfortunately a mugging is about more than a mobile. It's about kids feeling powerful in the street, having a sense of control. It's bullying. If I didn't feel so angry about muggers, I would feel sorry for them. Mugging is the only way they feel any satisfaction.

You may not be able to stop it happening, but there are precautions you can take.

● Don't carry a mobile when you can avoid it and make sure it is concealed when you do carry it.

● Walk confidently in the street. Police say that muggers look for potential victims and they are more likely to leave you alone if you look as if you own the street.

● Don't carry excess money. It will hurt more if they lift all your cash rather than just your bus fare.

● Don't carry games consoles unless you have to and unless they are very well concealed.

● Try to walk in a group rather than alone.

● Choose routes that are well lit and populated. Don't go for the short-cuts down alleys.

● If you think you are about to be assaulted, try yelling for help or bang on the nearest door. People don't usually do this, out of embarrassment, but attention is likely to scare muggers away.

● If you do get assaulted, don't fight back. Your attacker might have a knife.

● Do not wait around. The moment you can, phone 999 (probably on somebody else's mobile, if they have nicked yours!). The police now take street crime very seriously and if they have a description, they may well get a patrol car out to find them. If you leave it 10 or 15 minutes, your assailants will have disappeared.

If the police find the culprit, they are unlikely to bring charges if the incident has involved only verbal harassment. They are able to press charges if the mugger has searched you or stolen anything from you.

It's a horrible business. It can happen anywhere but it certainly does happen in the inner city and I think it's vile that there are kids growing up who do not feel safe in the streets, and other kids growing up to think that this is a way of getting what they want and getting away with it.

'I have been mugged about a dozen times since I started at secondary school. Luckily, when I hit 6 feet tall, it all stopped. That's not very helpful to you, I know, if you're rather shorter. It is scary but you can't let them win and make you stay at home or only travel with your parents. I think I got better at avoiding it and dealing with it.' NICHOLAS, 15

'It was a big shock coming to university. It's not secure like home. I have to shut up and double lock everything. You quickly learn that you never carry your laptop at night. You always have to conceal it. There were lots of robberies in the first week of term.' TIAN, 20

'Two out of the six of us who share a flat have been beaten up. One just because the bloke thought he'd given him a funny look. You have to look out for yourself, especially on your own at night.' IAN, 19

'I was mugged last summer. I had my dad's mobile on me because, of course, mine had no credit on it. When that got taken, I thought my dad would kill me, so I chased after the muggers and demanded it back. It wasn't sensible and I ended up getting hurt. My advice would be, don't chase after muggers. And don't take your phone out in public.' ALEXIS, 18

Dear Teenager,
34 HOW TO AVOID HAVING YOUR DRINK SPIKED

Date rape (or 'drug facilitated sexual assault', as the police now call it) is a thoroughly nasty phenomenon that appears to becoming more common. At parties, bars or clubs, someone slips a substance into a drink. The spiked drink makes its victim feels very relaxed and without inhibition. The perpetrator is then able to have sex with their victim. A few hours later, the victim may not recall very much at all of what has happened and evidence is very hard to come by. The commonly used drugs disappear from the body within 72 hours. It is without doubt rape because the victim has been rendered incapable of saying no. It also means that the sex is more likely to be unprotected, therefore leaving the victim open to disease or pregnancy.

There are three main drugs used for date rape. They are rohypnol, GBH and ketamine hydrochloride. For the most part, when they are added to a drink, you can't see them, smell them or taste them.

Rohypnol, which goes by street names including Roofies, R2, Forget-Me-Pill and Mexican Valium, used to be the most common one. It is a legal drug that is used for insomnia. Acting responsibly, the manufacturers have now introduced new pills so that when they are added to a drink they turn it a greeny-blue colour.

GBH is also known as Easy-Lay, E Z Lay, Liquid Ecstasy and Get-Her-To-Bed. It is an illegal drug. Its effects take hold after about 15 minutes and last for 3–6 hours without alcohol, but if mixed with alcohol or other drugs, can last for 72 hours. It induces euphoria, drowsiness and sometimes coma.

Ketamine has the street names Special K, Ket Kat, Make-Her-Mine and Super K. It is mostly used as a veterinary sedative but is also used as an anaesthetic in hospitals. It makes the user feel disassociated from all bodily sensations. It induces amnesia and coma. It takes 20 minutes for the effects to happen and lasts for about 3 hours.

If you think you may have been date raped because of what you remember, or how your body feels, or what people around you are saying, then report it quickly to the police while the drug might still be detected. Any kind of rape is dreadful and you should not suffer the consequences on your own and in silence.

But what can you do to avoid date rape? One option is that you can now buy a tester strip (you can purchase these on the internet),

> Most sexual assaults don't involve the drugs listed on page 94. They involve alcohol. Recent research concluded that one in three young women say they have been sexually assaulted after getting drunk.

which you dip into your drink to check it hasn't been tampered with. Personally, I don't think they are reliable and would not recommend them. Don't put your trust in something that may not work. If you feel in a position where date rape feels a distinct possibility, the best solution is to leave. Now.

Alternatively, you can take sensible precautions.
- Only drink from a sealed can or bottle. Do not accept open drinks from other people.
- Do not drink from a punch-type bowl of mixed drink.
- If you want to buy an open drink, buy it yourself directly from the bar and do not use any intermediaries.
- Staying sober is also a good defence. So too is using your instincts and not staying around people you don't entirely trust.
- Do not invite people you don't know well back to your room and don't go to theirs. Do not be trusting.

Rape can happen to men as well as to women.

'Looking out for drink-spiking has been hammered home to me by my mum. She's obsessed with it. Even every time she rings me up she reminds me. So it's ingrained in me. It is a massive problem. I had my drink spiked once and I've got friends it's happened to. I must have leant over to talk to someone, with my drink in my hand but not concentrating 100 per cent on it. I certainly hadn't put it down. I would never be stupid enough to leave a drink unattended and go back to it.' ALEXIS, 18

'One of my friends had her drink spiked. It's one of the things you learn: always watch your drink.' HANNAH, 20

 www.roofie.com is an organisation that researches drug-related rape and sexual abuse and offers advice on how to avoid drink-spiking.

Dear Teenager,
35 HOW TO HAVE YOUR BODY PIERCED

I am not writing this as an advocate of any kind of piercing, even though I have pierced ears. The older I get, the more I feel it's a good thing not to mess with your body if you don't have to. Any kind of piercing is an invasive procedure and carries risks. I am also a wimp. When I had my ears pierced in a major London department store, I thought it was an excruciating experience. I stood up and tried to walk away. Instead I fainted and collapsed in a heap on the floor of the jewellery department. I then had gunk coming out of my ear lobes for nearly a year. Now that the memory of the agony has faded, I wear earrings all the time.

It is illegal to tattoo anyone under the age of 18 but there are no legal age restrictions on piercing. The legislation that governs the industry is not as clear or as tight as it should be. Anyone with a hammer and nail can set themselves up to do body piercing. The only form of piercing that can be regulated currently is ear piercing. Any trustworthy body piercer will be registered as an ear piercer.

● If you choose to have a piercing, go to a dedicated practitioner who is registered and has the necessary certificates.

● Have a look round to check that it is clean and the instruments are sterilised. Satisfy yourself that the conditions are hygienic. If they are not, you are increasing the risk of blood-borne diseases such as hepatitis and HIV.

● If a piercer says they will do the job straight away, leave. There should always be a cooling off period. At festivals, there are often piercers with mobile vehicles but, even there, they send customers away for a few hours after their enquiry.

● If anyone wants to use an ear piercing gun on any other part of your anatomy, leave. A gun up your nose can pierce the septum. It is designed for the ear lobe alone.

● You should be asked for full personal details and medical history.

HEALING TIMES FOR COMMON PIERCINGS

Ear 3–4 months
Lip 1–2 months
Navel 1–24 months
Nipple 2–6 months
Nose 2–3 months
Tongue 1–2 months

- If you want a body piercing, go to an established body piercer, not an ear piercer. They are much more likely to know what they are doing.

- Think hard before you have a body piercing. Areas of the body which have lots of blood vessels (such as the tongue) may lead to serious blood loss. Tongue piercing also carries a high risk of bacterial infection because of the number of bacteria present in the mouth.

- Genital piercing makes me shudder. It sounds like mutilation to me. In an American study on intimate piercings, 66 per cent of people with nipple piercings and 52 per cent of those with genital piercings developed medical problems. The vast majority suffered in silence and failed to get medical advice.

- If you are of school age, remember that there may be school regulations banning piercing. Consult your parents too. They may have strong feelings about it.

- Make sure you are given good after-care advice. If the area becomes infected, seek medical advice.

'My mum wouldn't let me have piercings. So I went out on my 16th birthday and had my ears pierced. Two weeks after my 18th birthday I had two more ear piercings. I'd like to have my tummy done but I am a chicken and so many things can go wrong.' JOCASTA, 18

 www.youngwomenshealth.org/body-piercing.html
offers good advice about how to heal piercings.

Dear Teenager,
36 HOW TO HAVE A TATTOO SAFELY

Tattoos aren't allowed by law until you're 18. That doesn't stop some illegal operators from tattooing minors. Unfortunately they are not likely to be reputable tattooists who know what they are doing and follow the best hygiene guidelines, so beware.

I'm a bit squeamish about needles so the idea of tattooing really doesn't appeal to me much. Others less squeamish than me have joined the popular trend for adding peek-a-boo tattoos to different parts of their anatomy. When I was growing up it was mostly sailors and builders who had them down their arms and across their chests but now you see cute little designs popping up in the small of people's backs or their shoulders or their ankles. We can't know for certain how many people have them and how many remove them but one skin doctor reckons 50 per cent of people regret their tattoos. Getting tattoos removed is not trivial. It is much harder and more expensive than having one done.

A tattoo is a permanent design made of dye injected into your dermis. That's the layer of skin below the epidermis, the top layer of skin that flakes away and is replaced regularly. An electronic needle drills down very fast and leaves a deposit of dye in the hole it has punctured. It moves along repeating the action rather like a sewing machine. The dye lasts for a lifetime.

Just as with piercing (see **How to Have Your Body Pierced**), hygiene is all-important. A tattooist is dealing with blood and serious infections can easily be passed through needles or sprayed blood from client to client. There are no known cases of the transmission of AIDS through tattooing but there have been cases of hepatitis and other infections. You do not want to endanger your life for a body decoration, so take care who you choose to do this for you.

- Choose a studio where you are sure they are using an autoclave, a steam-powered sterilising unit.
- Make sure the studio looks clean.
- Ask for the tattooist's professional memberships.
- Make sure the tattooist is using gloves.
- Ask if he or she is using new needles (check the packet).

● Make sure you understand about aftercare before you leave.

Tattoo removal

If you want to have a tattoo removed, you'll have to pay for it yourself. The cost depends on the scale of the job, but if it costs you £40 to put it on, it will probably set you back around £600 to remove it.

These days most removals are done by laser surgery. It usually requires lots of sessions. Black and red inks are the easiest to remove. Green and other mixed colours will never be removed by laser applications. Some tattoos can take up to a year to be lasered to a faint mark. It is very difficult to remove a tattoo completely.

Even if you change your mind about the little dragon curling round your shoulder blade you can probably live with it. You may feel quite differently about carrying round the name of the love of your life who is now your ex. If one in three marriages fails, the odds aren't in favour of tattooing a name onto your body!

www.embarrassingproblems.com for useful information about tattoos.

- -

Dear Teenager,
37 HOW TO STOP BULLIES

If you are the victim of bullying, you feel weak and worthless and when you feel like that it is hard to do anything about it.

Bullying comes in lots of forms. It can be verbal abuse based on a person's characteristics or race. It can be physical. It can be about pushing someone into doing actions they would rather not do. Or it can be a matter of exclusion, preventing someone from being a part of a group. Peer pressure is a form of bullying too. If all your friends get drunk or take drugs and pester you to do the same, then that's a form of bullying also.

Bullying is not exclusive to children. Lots of adults get bullied too. They have to learn how to assert themselves and stop the bullies getting their way. If you learn how to cope with bullies when you are a teenager, you'll be great at curbing any bullying tendencies of bosses at work. Here are some strategies to help you cope if you are a victim of bullies.

- Don't keep quiet. Get help. Tell someone what is going on.

- Your school will have an anti-bullying policy. Check it out and see what needs to happen. Take the policy to a teacher.

- Schools may have policies but they don't always act upon them. If you are unhappy about what's happening, or don't think you're being taken seriously, or simply don't know what to do, phone the professionals. Call ChildLine. They will give you specific advice regarding your situation. They'll help you decide what to say and to whom to say it.

- ChildLine recommends keeping a bullying diary. It is much easier to round up the evidence if you keep a note. They have an excellent model of a diary on their website.

'Lots of my friends get drunk all the time and they expect me to do the same. They make me feel a reject when I don't do it.' GEMMA, 16

 www.childline.org.uk or ring their phone line for direct advice on **0800 1111**.
www.kidscape.org.uk for more advice on how to cope with bullies.

Dear Teenager,
38 HOW TO BE SAFE ON THE INTERNET

The internet is no safer or more dangerous than any other form of communication. The main reason children are sometimes not safe on the internet is because they spend so much more time on computers than their parents, and their parents don't have a clue about what they are doing and have never established basic guidelines. There are basic safety rules, which both parents and children should know.

Fundamentally, it's all common sense. It's about not doing things in the cyber world that you would not do in the real one.

The internet is a wonderful resource for teenagers. Not just for working, and not just for playing either. It's a fantastic tool of communication. My kids have a much richer and broader social life than I did at their age because they keep so many relationships going by email or instant messaging.

Come what may, using the World Wide Web you will be exposed to some pretty nasty and irritating pop ups with lewd shots. Their degree of lewdness sometimes surprises me. Twelve per cent of internet sites are pornographic. Most people just regard these as a nuisance, disregard them and carry on. It goes without saying that you should hit the exit button.

Some basic dos and don'ts

● Download whatever filtering software is available from your internet provider. Use a firewall. Download anti-spyware software.

● Never open attachments from unknown senders. Delete them unopened. They might contain a virus.

● In chat rooms, don't give out personal details or information that could enable other people to trace you.

● Do not believe that anyone on the net is who they say they are. You must have read stories about people lured to meet others they have encountered on the internet who turn out to be violent 50 year olds instead of the 17 year olds they purported to be. Do not arrange to meet anyone you only know through the net.

● If you are worried by the tone or nature of any chat room discussion, leave it. If it is unpleasant or bullying you should also report it to your internet moderator and editor.

● If you are under 18, avoid over-18s chat rooms.

● Never visit racist or pornographic sites. If you fall into one by accident, tell your parents so that they don't start thinking you have been corrupted.

● If you are buying something using the internet, be alert. There is a huge amount of internet fraud. Merchandise may never arrive or not be what you expect it to be. Always check out the seller as much as you are able and look at any feedback ratings. Do not do business with someone who will not give you a real address and contact details. Do not give out your credit card details unless you feel completely confident about the seller.

'Viruses can ruin your computer or destroy your hard-drive, so only download things from trustworthy places. My friend had his coursework wiped when he downloaded a song, so it does happen!

Mum is hopeless about the internet. She gets nervous when I'm in chat rooms.' NICHOLAS, 15

Dear Parents,

Parents do panic a lot about internet safety and there is plenty of security software you can buy if you want to. On the whole, the best protection is simply to make sure you teach your child the dos and don'ts early on and keep the internet a family activity and not a secretive one. People are entitled to keep their emails private but you should worry if chat rooms are only entered behind closed doors. You can check the history folder of your browser as it contains a list of recently visited sites. If you see a porn site there, don't freak out, it may have been visited by accident.

I couldn't live without my computer now. When it's not working, it's as if I have had a limb amputated. I find it hard to credit that such a short time ago computers were not a part of our lives. Nevertheless, you can have too much of a good thing. We have constant arguments about time spent in front of the screen. My view, disputed by all my family, is that you shouldn't be on it right up to bedtime. This is because you should relax and wind down before sleep. This is true of any age and applies as much to adults as to children and teenagers.

Dear Teenager,
39 HOW TO KEEP YOUR MOBILE PHONE SAFE

There are more than 56 million mobile phones in the UK, and the number is rising. Quite often nowadays, people have two or three of them for business and personal use. People start carrying them younger and younger. They are a fashion accessory and people will pay a small fortune for the latest all-singing, all-dancing model. Naturally, they are frequently stolen. Fifty per cent of all street crime involves mobiles. In London (there are no national statistics available) 40 per cent of victims are under 21. Given these facts, it is absurd that most people fail to register their mobiles with the police database.

If the police arrest someone, they can check their mobile against the register. If it is your phone and you have registered it, they will see that it is stolen.

You need to go to *www.immobilise.com* and register your details. You need to find your IMEI number, which is a 14–17 digit number unique to your phone. To find this, dial *#06# (STAR/HASH/06/HASH) and your IMEI number will appear automatically. Also, if you take the battery out of the phone and look at the label inside, you will see the same number. If it is not the same, your phone is probably one that has previously been stolen.

If your mobile is stolen, call your network provider to let them know what has happened and they will block the phone. You can find the number for all network providers on the Immobilise website or contact Immobilise direct. If you have an insurance policy, you will need to report the incident to the police and to your insurers.

If you lose your phone, you lose it. But at least make it harder for a criminal to use it. Encourage your parents and family to register their phones too.

Don't forget that carrying a mobile makes you a target for muggers. (See **How to Not Be Mugged**.) Always try to keep your mobile concealed.

 www.immobilise.com for registering your phone details. Or call them on **08701 123 123**.

Dear Teenager,
40 HOW TO CALL EMERGENCY SERVICES

Before you put in the call, make sure you know your location and phone number. This can be difficult if you are on a car journey and don't know the name of the road. Try to think clearly about where you are, which junction of the motorway you may just have left or which town you have passed through and look for any local landmarks.

When you ring 999 the first person you will speak to will be the telephone operator, who will ask you which service you require. State which service you need (Fire, Police or Ambulance). You will hear a ringing tone while they connect you to the right service.

You will then be asked for the name or number of your house or building; the road name; the town or village name. Try to be as precise as possible, and speak clearly. Try not to rush. As soon as the location of the incident is known, the police, fire or ambulance people will be sent. Do not hang up. The controller will then ask you some questions about the incident. This does not delay the help, which is already on its way. The call taker may be able to offer you advice that will allow you to help until the relevant service arrives.

A CALL FOR HELP
Two-and-a-half million 999 calls are made each year to the Metropolitan Police. In fact, only about 20 per cent of these actually require an emergency response. This is what some 'emergency' callers are reported to have said:

Do you know a good stain remover?
There's a rat in my kitchen.
I can't turn my tap off.
I think my neighbour is a spy.
I think I've found some stolen property.
My bike's been stolen.
I was in a traffic accident yesterday.

ICE

A scheme has been launched to encourage people to put ICE (which stands for In Case of Emergency) on their mobiles. Under the heading ICE, you enter the number of your next of kin. Then, if you are involved in an accident, the emergency services can browse your numbers and know whom to call. For young people the ICE should probably be a parent. If you want to list more than one, put ICE1 and ICE2. The idea was initiated by the East Anglian Ambulance Service and has now been picked up nationwide.

Keep a look out for the emergency services to arrive. If possible ask someone to stand outside to guide them to the incident. If it is dark, put lights on so that you stand out. Most of all, try to stay calm.

Happily, the majority of us don't have to call the emergency services very often. The average person rings for an ambulance once every seven years. The trouble then is, when you do need to call, and you're freaked out by an accident or crime, it's hard to remember what the procedure is.

You only call 999 in an emergency. One of my children, then aged four, once called 999 to alert the police to the fact that a garden pot had been stolen overnight from outside the front door. I was in the bath when he made the call and, shortly afterwards, in my bath towel, had to confront two police officers looking for the emergency.

At the other extreme, when one of my children was mugged on his way home from school, we only called the local police half-an-hour later and the officer said we should have phoned 999 straightaway because the muggers may still have been in the area. You must always call 999 for the police if you are in immediate danger or a crime is happening now.

The emergency services receive lots of hoax and unnecessary calls. This of course clogs up the system and slows down the response speed. Sometimes, emergency calls are made accidentally by mobile phones squashed into bags or pockets.

It may sometimes be hard to know when to call an ambulance. When the following medical conditions occur, you must call: chest pain, difficulty in breathing, loss of consciousness, severe loss of blood, choking, fitting or convulsions, drowning or severe allergic reactions. If you are uncertain and need help, call anyway. If the situation is not an emergency but you want advice, call NHS Direct (see **How to Know if You Are Ill**.)

Even if your mobile phone has no credit on it, you can still use it to make a 999 call.

'If someone harasses you in the street, call 999. Don't think it's not worth bothering about. It is.' NICHOLAS, 15

Dear Teenager,
41 HOW TO COPE IF YOU ARE ARRESTED

If you get arrested, stay calm. Know your rights and try to keep a clear head about what is going on.

- If the police come to your house, ask to see their identification. Ask them which station they come from, and phone the station to check they are who they say. Ask why you are being arrested. (If the police are looking for drugs, you may be handcuffed straightaway and may not have the opportunity to call the station. This is to stop evidence being destroyed.)

- If the police have a warrant, they have the right to enter and to search. They don't have to put things back the way they found them. They will issue you with their warrant, details of their powers and a copy of any property seized.

- If you are taken to a police station, give your name and address. The police can ask for fingerprints, photos and saliva samples, which you are also obliged to give. These can be kept on file even if you are not charged.

- Any valuables you have on you will be removed and logged. This includes your mobile phone.

● At the police station the police must serve you with a written notice setting out your rights. This includes the fact that you can ask for a solicitor. If you do not know one, you can ask for the duty solicitor whose services will be free. Whether you are under arrest or have gone to the police station voluntarily, you are entitled to a solicitor.

● You are entitled to one phone call (unless there is reason to believe that you might tip off other suspects or interfere with evidence). Let someone responsible know where you are and why.

● You must be given regular breaks for food and drink and you must not be subjected to unreasonable pressure.

● If you are under 17, the police are not allowed to interview you without an 'appropriate adult' being present. This is usually someone unconnected with the incident being investigated. You could ask for an older sibling. Otherwise the police have their own panel of appropriate adults and will provide one for you.

● Once an officer has reason to believe that you have committed an offence, they must caution you by explaining that it may harm your defence if you do not mention when questioned something which you later rely on in court. Anything you do say may be given in evidence.

● You do not have to speak. Even though your failure to answer questions can be held against you, you cannot be convicted solely because you have failed to answer questions in a police interview. The best advice is usually to remain silent until you have met with a solicitor.

● You have to be released or go before a magistrate within 36 hours.

I've never been arrested but it sounds no fun at all. Lawyers tell me the best practice is to be calm, polite and to speak as little as possible. No comment, until your solicitor says otherwise.

If you get taken to a police station, just answer the questions directly. Don't volunteer information. If a policeman says, 'Where did you come from?', say 'I'm coming from my girlfriend's' (or wherever). Don't say 'I'm coming from my girlfriend's and we were hanging out with her brother and his mates...' Don't answer back aggressively. I get stopped a lot. Black people do. A few months ago I got stopped by a policeman. He said, 'Where's the ganga?' I'm a black Rasta and they just won't believe I don't smoke. Then one policeman said, 'I know him. I've seen him on the telly.' And they started to be nice. If you think you've been stopped unfairly, make a note of the policeman's number and make an official complaint. I've done that.

BENJAMIN ZEPHANIAH, POET AND NOVELIST

www.adviceguide.org is the website for the Citizens Advice Bureau and has a good section on young people and crime.

Dear Teenager,
42 HOW TO GET INSURANCE

Insurance is a business about risk. An insurance premium is the contribution people pay to a company in case an unfortunate event happens. If it does, the idea is that using the pool of money from all the contributions received, the insurance company will compensate you for the incident. If nothing happens, they get to keep the cash. If you are in a high-risk group, you will be liable to higher premiums and have to pay more. If you are in a low-risk group, you will be charged less.

When you are choosing insurance, you should always read the small print very carefully. Here are some of the things you need to look out for.

● **Excess charge:** This is the amount you have to contribute yourself before the insurers pay up the rest of the claim.

● **What exactly is covered?** It is no good just assuming that your insurance will cover you whatever happens. You may well find that the policy has low limits that may not be adequate to cover your costs.

● **Exemptions:** You may find that your policy does not cover skiing or water sports, or using your car for business, or is only applicable to people over a certain age.

● **New for old:** Some policies only cover you for the current value of an item you have lost. So if you have a TV stolen and it was five years old, they will only pay out the value of the actual TV you had. It's much better (though more expensive) to buy a new for old policy so that you are able to afford to replace the goods.

There are many different types of insurance, but here are some of the ones you are most likely to come across.

Travel insurance

● Make sure you take out cover for the whole time you are going to be away, whether it is for a weekend or a year.

● Make sure your insurance covers medical care (for if you fall ill or have an accident) including repatriating you; and theft (for if you have items or money lost or stolen).

● Shop around but beware going for the cheapest option in case it does not give you adequate cover.

● Look at your policy and take a note of the 24-hour emergency number so that you know where to find it when you need it.

● Do not go away without insurance. Many people do, and they regret it. (See **How to Have a Good Gap Year.**)

● If you are travelling in Europe, take your EHIC card (previously known as E111). You can apply for one online or through the Post Office. It entitles you to medical cover locally. This does not replace insurance cover.

Car insurance

● If you drive a car you need to be covered by car insurance. You can be covered on your parents' insurance (although their premiums will go up; see **How to Drive a Car**) or if you own a car you can take out your own.

● If you're driving an old banger you may decide to take out third party, fire and theft insurance only. Then if anything happens to the car that is your fault, you are not covered for the damage to it. If you have a posh car that you care for, you will need the full insurance and if you are under 25 you will find that you are penalised heavily. And if you're male (and therefore statistically the most likely to have an accident) you'll probably have to take out a sizeable loan to pay it!

House and contents insurance

● House insurance covers structural damage to your bricks and mortar and fixtures and fittings. If you are living as a tenant in private or college accommodation, this should be covered for you. You are, however, usually responsible for your contents insurance. It is very unwise not to have it.

● A contents policy covers damage to property from fire or flood as well as theft. When looking for a policy, check whether you are covered for items outside your home. What happens for example if you lose your handbag or you have an item stolen when you are staying away from home?

● If you have something stolen, report it to the police, who will give you a reference number. The insurance company will require this.

It feels rough having to part with money for nothing tangible but if your holiday gets cancelled or your house catches fire, you'll be very pleased when the insurance company pays out.

 www.nusonline.co.uk (National Union of Students website) has a section about insurance. It recommends Endsleigh Insurance for students.
www.dh.gov.uk/travellers is the website for applying for the EHIC card (the replacement for the E111).

SEX AND DRUGS

SEX AND DRUGS ARE STILL THE BIG TABOO area for most families. It may be OK discussing these matters in theory but when it comes down to what you've been getting up to and with whom, things can get heated pretty quickly.

There are also no right or wrong answers about what's OK and what's not, for you. I think, however, there are three guiding principles for both sex and drugs, which should help you decide what to do.

The first is that you must be very aware of the power of peer pressure and be resistant to it. Just because everyone else is smoking, or getting laid, or drinking alcohol or taking Ecstasy, there is no reason for you to do the same. You have to be able to stand by your own decisions for your own reasons. Peer pressure is a form of bullying.

(continued overleaf)

MINI QUIZ

Are you better equipped than your parents to answer the following questions?

1. For how many hours is the morning-after pill effective?
2. Is cannabis legal?
3. At what age can you drink alcohol in a pub restaurant?
4. What is the age of consent?

Answers

1. 72 hours, but it is most effective within 24.
2. Cannabis is a Class C drug. It is illegal.
3. 16, as long as you're eating a proper meal.
4. 16 (17 in Northern Ireland).

The second principle is that you need to recognise the risks you are taking by acting illegally. It may seem easy to trade dope outside the school gates but if you get caught you can be in serious trouble. Do you want to start your working life with a criminal conviction? If you're still going to do it, make sure you know the possible consequences so that you can minimise the risks.

Which leads on to the last principle: inform yourself. If you know about STIs (sexually transmitted infections) and AIDS, drugs and the law, sex and pregnancy, you'll be much better placed to take a decision about what's right for you.

Dear Teenager,
43 HOW TO HAVE SEX LEGALLY

If you are planning on having sex, you should know what the law is. Even though it is not legal for under-16s to have sex, nearly a third of them do. The age of consent for heterosexual and homosexual men and women is now 16 in England, Wales and Scotland, and 17 in Northern Ireland.

● Even if parents say it is OK for their 15-year-old son or daughter to have sex, it is still unlawful.

● Anyone aged over 18 who has sex with someone under 16 is committing a sex offence.

● Anyone having sex with a child under the age of 13 is committing rape.

● If someone under the age of 16 is sexually involved with someone over 16, the younger person will not be committing an offence. The older person will.

● You should wait to have sex until you are legally old enough, and until you are ready. But whenever you have sex, make sure it's safe sex.

Discussing sex with your parents is pretty embarrassing but the sooner you get in the habit of doing it, the easier it is, for you and for them. You could try getting a few library books (there are some pretty good reference books now, which are entertaining and informative). You are likely to get more straight talking from a book than from most parents. Wet dreams, periods, masturbation, birth control, AIDS, homosexuality, the law … these are all things you need to know about (not just have a vague notion). A good way of introducing the subject is by reading the papers, which are full of sex one way or another. It's good to be able to talk to parents about sex in case you ever really need to. And anyway, presumably they know something about the subject, if they have got you.

'Where I live now, sex and drugs aren't taboo subjects. If the girls were at a rave and got into trouble, or their friends did, they'd call their mum and tell her. I would never, ever, have done that. It may be embarrassing or humiliating for parents to talk about it, but you've got to if you want to protect your kids. There are more STIs than ever, and drugs are ridiculously cheap.' KACHENGA, 19

 This is really embarrassing because I always say I know everything and I'm the man. But once, I had a deal with a girl that we'd have sex together. Only it had to be the right time. This girl explained that girls have a thing called a period. For a few days each month, she said, they had a time when they didn't have a period. In other words, she reversed it. So every time I asked if it was the right time she said, 'I'm on my period,' and 'I wasn't on for a few days but you missed it.' For months I thought, I've got to wait until she hasn't got a period. I occasionally see her now and I think *****!

BENJAMIN ZEPHANIAH, POET AND NOVELIST

www.adviceguide.com is the website for the Citizens Advice Bureau and lays out clearly the legalities regarding sex.

Dear Parents,

Research shows that parents today overwhelmingly believe in the benefits of talking openly about sex to their children. But the research also shows that in fact they hardly address the issue at all. There is a massive gulf between what they believe to be good and what they actually do. Most of us have got beyond the gooseberry bush stage, but have you discussed with your sons how easy it is to get a girl pregnant and what precautions they should take? And have you discussed with your sons and daughters what precautions they should take against AIDS?

Children from households in which sex is discussed openly are no more likely to start having sexual relations sooner. So get talking!

Dear Teenager,
44 HOW TO NOT GET PREGNANT

Of course, the only sure way to not get pregnant is not to have sex.

If you are going to have sex, make sure it's safe sex. You don't want a baby and you don't want a sexual disease. One-third of under-16s in Britain are sexually active and nearly 8,000 of them get pregnant each year. This is the highest rate of teenage pregnancy in Western Europe.

- Don't do it when you're drunk. Don't do it unless you are sure you want to. Make sure you are using adequate contraception and make sure that you use a condom to prevent the spread of sexual disease.

- Contraceptives are obtainable for free from a GP or clinic. You don't have to be 16. You can also buy condoms in supermarkets and chemists. Using a condom stops most STIs. You can use a condom as well as another method of contraception such as the pill. (See the section on **How to Get Contraceptives.**) Don't let embarrassment get in the way of fixing yourself up with the right contraception.

● If you are a girl and have had sex without contraception, go to your chemist or doctor or family planning clinic or Brook Advisory Clinic and ask for the morning-after pill, which is effective up to 72 hours after sex but is more effective the earlier it is used.

● If you have any worries about either being pregnant or having a sexually transmitted infection (STI), for goodness sake, go and see a doctor. Doctors are obliged by law to talk to you in confidence irrespective of your age. They will not tell your parents unless there are exceptional circumstances and they have grave concerns for your welfare. If you go to a clinic, you won't have to risk talking to the family GP. Your visit will also be in complete confidence.

● To find your nearest clinic, check the phone book under sexual health. It may also be listed under GUM (Genito-Urinary Medicine), STD (Sexually Transmitted Diseases); or STI (Sexually Transmitted Infections). Sexual Health clinics are normally based at local hospitals. You can book an appointment without giving your real name and the treatment will be free.

● If you think you may be pregnant and want to arrange an abortion, contact your GP, family planning clinic or Brook Advisory Clinic. Don't wait because you can't face up to the consequences. Far better to go and talk to someone who understands your predicament and will offer you professional advice.

'When you move into a flat share and you go out with a guy, there's no one to keep an eye out on whether you've come home. After a while, my flatmates and I got to know one another better and now we always check up with each other and see if we're staying the night at home or somewhere else.' MATILDA, 20

'It's nice being able to go and see your girlfriend without worrying about what her mum will say.' TIAN, 20

'I'm gay, and it would have been so helpful if my parents had been prepared to talk about sex. Not the mechanics but the emotions of it. And relationships. I could never tell them anything. I was living a double life.' KACHENGA, 19

'I was never taught anything at home because sex was a strictly forbidden topic. Most of the time I find out things through the media. Friends have also been very helpful. Major problems such as pregnancy would definitely leave me shattered. Friends would probably be the first ones I turn to. Although the college provides a welfare service I doubt if I would trust them enough.' ASHLEIGH, 18

The brightest girl in my year got pregnant. She threw it all away. Don't do it. Don't run under a bus. Don't get pregnant.
FIONA SHAW, ACTRESS
(AUNT PETUNIA IN THE *HARRY POTTER* FILMS)

Dear Parents,

There comes a point with your teenager when you can no longer control them, no longer organise their lives for them the way you would like them to be. They are their own people but they are still teenagers so they are likely to be wayward and cussed. You can see what's right or wrong for them but they refuse to oblige. So your teenage son/daughter is sleeping with a 30 year old you don't like or trust, what are you going to do about it? You can't physically restrain them. If you ban them from the house or drive them away, it's not going to improve things. You can make it clear how you feel about the situation and you can lay down some ground rules, but on the whole it is better for you to know what is going on and to be there when they need you than it is to drive the same wayward behaviour underground. Parents of teenagers are sometimes put in intolerable situations, especially when it comes to sex and drugs. Know that you are not the only ones suffering and that it is only a stage that they are going through (you hope!). Try to keep the lines of communication open and remember that you

(continued overleaf)

need a life too. You can give them all the love and guidance in the world but there comes a point when they have to take responsibility for themselves. Don't be so wound up by what they are doing that you end up without a life yourself.

And, don't forget, when they are arguing with you, they are trying to shock you, trying to test the boundaries, trying to wind you up. That's their job…

Dear Teenager,
45 HOW TO AVOID SEXUALLY TRANSMITTED INFECTIONS

Sexually transmitted infections or STIs can be caused by bacteria or viruses and move across from one person to their partner when they have sex. They thrive in the genital areas. You only need to have sex once to contract an infection but the more sexual partners you have, the more you increase your chances of getting an STI. A condom is the best protection.

STIs are very common. Some people have no symptoms and therefore don't know that they have an infection. Other people feel considerable discomfort. Most STIs can be sorted with medication and cause no long-term damage but some, like HIV, are very dangerous. Most STIs are treatable with antibiotics.

These are some of the STIs you could catch if you don't use a condom.

- Chlamydia (the highest rate of infection occurs in girls aged 15–19). Men often don't know they have got it; it can make women infertile.
- Gonorrhoea (sometimes called the clap).
- Genital herpes (once infected, you can control it but not eradicate it).
- Genital warts (probably the commonest STI on the globe).

 25 per cent of sexually active teenagers pick up an STI each year.

HOW TO PROTECT YOURSELF AGAINST STIs

Prevention is far more desirable than cure. All of these STIs are much harder to catch if you use a condom. Condoms can't always prevent the spread of warts, which might be present in a larger area than the bit the condom covers, but (apart from not having sex) they are the best way of protecting yourself against all sexually transmitted infections.

Don't believe that your partner couldn't possibly be infected because they say they are not or because they have no symptoms. They can still be carriers even if they don't know it.

Don't think it is sufficient that you are using some other form of contraception. If you or your partner is on the pill, use a condom too. This is called 'double Dutch'.

If you are a girl and you are having sex, you should also sign up for smear testing. This is a test in which the nurse or doctor scrapes a few cells from your cervix and sends them off to the lab for testing. I can't say it's a pleasant experience; the instrument they use, called a speculum, always feels hideously cold but the discomfort of a few seconds is well worth it for your health.

If you have any unusual symptoms, seek help right away.

- Trichomoniasis (sometimes called trich; only causes symptoms in women).
- HIV (can be passed by heterosexual as well as homosexual sex and through drug users sharing needles).
- Hepatitis B (like HIV, this infection can be spread through sex or shared needles).
- Syphilis.

Here are some of the possible symptoms of STI for both sexes:
- Pain or burning sensations when peeing
- Itching
- Discharge from the penis or vagina

- Pain or swelling
- Sores or white patches in the mouth
- Pain when having sex.

These symptoms may have nothing to do with STIs but you must get them checked out straight away.

You can go to your GP or you can go to your local STI clinic (sometimes called a Genito-Urinary Medicine or GUM clinic). These will be listed in your phone directory under STD (Sexually Transmitted Diseases) or Genito-Urinary. An STI clinic will treat you in complete confidence. Don't be too embarrassed to go.

www.brook.org.uk for more advice about STIs.

Dear Teenager,
46 HOW TO GET CONTRACEPTIVES

You can get contraceptives (including condoms) from your GP or your local family planning clinic or Brook Advisory Clinic and they will cost you nothing. You can also buy condoms and emergency contraceptive pills from the chemist.

There are myriad forms of contraception that suit different people according to their age and their lifestyle. What suits you now may well be different from what suits you in ten years. Unfortunately no form of contraception is perfect but they are all much better than an unwanted pregnancy. It seems a perverse act of nature that when you are at your most fertile (in your teens) you are least likely to want a baby. So if you decide to have sex, don't rely on luck, get the right form of contraception for you. You may be embarrassed. You may be under-age. Don't let these things stop you from getting contraception. Crossing your fingers is the lousiest form of contraception in the world.

Whatever form of contraception you go for, you should be using a condom too. Chances are you will have more than one sexual partner in your life and no other form of contraception stops the spread of sexually transmitted infections. If you are a girl, there are many options to consider, including the following.

- You can choose the pill. The combined pill is 99 per cent effective (if used properly). It prevents the egg from being released by the ovaries each month. You take a pill a day with a break of one week. Or there is the progestogen-only pill. This too is 99 per cent effective, but you have to take the pill at the same time every day, which can be a nightmare.

- You can use a diaphragm or cap. These are called barrier methods. You pop a device into the vagina before sex, along with some spermicide, and remove it after sex. These are slightly less effective than the pill.

- You can have an IUD (intra-uterine device, sometimes called the coil) or an IUS (intra-uterine system) fitted by the doctor. Once fitted, it can stay there for five years unless you want to remove it sooner.

- You can have a contraceptive patch, which you stick on your skin (a bit like a smoker's patch) or a contraceptive implant just below the skin in your upper arm. The implant lasts three years.

- If you have had unprotected sex, then there is emergency contraception available. If you go to your doctor within five days, they can fit an IUD (which will also give you continued protection). Alternatively, you can take the morning-after pill, available from a doctor or the chemist. This is most effective if you take it within 12 hours (95 per cent effective), but you can take it up to 72 hours after sex although its effectiveness drops to 58 per cent.

How well a contraceptive works is very much determined by your ability to follow the instructions to the letter. You can't be on the pill and forget to take it every couple of nights and expect it to be effective.

Most of the research and effort regarding contraceptives, apart from the condom, falls to the girl, but it should also be a matter of great concern to the boy too. Don't rush into it without thinking. You probably don't want either a baby or a sexually transmitted infection right now.

 www.brook.org.uk for free and confidential sex, contraception and abortion advice for young people.

Dear Teenager,

47 HOW TO KNOW MORE ABOUT DRUGS THAN YOUR PARENTS

This one is easy for many people because their parents don't know much about drugs, and if their parents do know anything it is probably well out of date. The strength of drugs, the availability of them and what we know about their effects have all changed over the years.

People take drugs for lots of different reasons. Some go through a period of experimenting. Others try drugs once. Smaller numbers use them recreationally. Some drug users end up having serious life-affecting problems: with the law, with their health, their social life and with debt. The trouble is, before you start you don't know which group you will end up in.

Taking drugs is criminal behaviour that can land you in serious trouble. If you are buying illegal drugs you can also never be sure what it is you are buying. Some of the side-effects are horrible and you may also be damaging your health. Some drugs can kill. Illegal drugs kill about 2,500 people a year in Britain and seriously harm the health and well-being of many thousands more.

You have to decide for yourself what your view is on drugs. Whether you think you will never take them or you do take them already, you should know as much as possible about what you may be offered. Drugs come in so many different shapes and forms that they are sometimes hard to recognise. Some even look like sweets. There are three basic drug groups. The first are those that are central nervous system depressants (such as alcohol, and heroin); the second are stimulants (such as cocaine and Ecstasy); and the third are hallucinogens (such as LSD and mushrooms and ketamine). Sharing needles to inject drugs puts you at risk of HIV/AIDS and hepatitis.

Here are some basics about the drugs you might come across and what they look like.

● **LSD** (*acid, trips, tabs, blotters, microdots, dots*): This comes as tiny squares of paper that are swallowed. LSD is a hallucinogenic. People see things more brightly and objects and time become distorted. The effects are known as 'trips' and there can be good trips or bad trips and bad ones can be terrifying. Once a trip has started it cannot be stopped. LSD is a Class A drug.

- **Cannabis** *(marijuana, hash, shit, ash, ganja, skunk, spliff, wacky baccy, draw, blow, weed, puff, pot):* It comes as a brown lump, as dried leaves and buds or as an oil. You can smoke it, eat it or dunk it in tea. It makes you intoxicated or 'stoned'; a very relaxed feeling. It often makes people talk a lot, but it can cause some people to withdraw into themselves. It is sometimes seen as a 'cool', harmless drug, but emerging research suggests there may be a link between cannabis and mental health problems. It is currently classified as a Class C drug.

- **Tranquillisers** *(tranx, benzos, moggies, jellies, temazzies, eggs, valium, diazepam, mogadon):* Tranquillisers are usually tablets or capsules. You swallow them, or sometimes inject them. They can have a calming effect. They are sometimes prescribed legally by doctors (to reduce anxiety) and are said to be the cause of the nation's biggest hidden addiction problem. When they are prepared illegally for injecting, they are a Class A drug.

- **Crack and cocaine** *(stones, bones, wash, freebase, coke, Charlie, snow, C):* Crack comes as small, off-white rocks or lumps. It can be smoked in a pipe or in a spliff or heated in tin foil. Cocaine comes as white powder that is snorted up the nose or sometimes dissolved and injected. The drug has an impact very quickly, lasts less than half an hour (but stays in your system for three days) and is often very expensive. It can make you feel energetic and confident, but can cause heart attacks, anxiety and damage your nose. Crack and cocaine are Class A drugs.

- **Heroin** *(smack, brown, gear):* Heroin comes from the opium poppy and is a white or brown powder. It is sniffed, smoked (chased) or injected. It can also come as a clear liquid in a glass ampoule (amps), which is injected or swallowed. It is a very good physical and emotional painkiller and makes you feel warm and relaxed. You can easily overdose on heroin. It is a Class A drug.

- **Ketamine** *(K, CK and Calvin Klein when mixed with cocaine):* Comes as a pill, powder or liquid. It is swallowed, snorted or injected. It causes changes in perception similar to LSD and reduces feeling in the body, but can also suppress heart function and cause panic attacks. It is a Class A drug.

● **Solvents** *(glue):* Solvents are found in lighter fuel, hair spray, deodorant, nail varnish remover, glue and some paints and make you feel light-headed. They are inhaled or sniffed (huffing, tooting). It is illegal to sell butane lighter fuel to anyone under 18. Solvents are very dangerous and can kill after one use.

● **Ecstasy** *(E, Doves, XTC, disco biscuits, echoes, hug drug, burgers, fantasy):* Ecstasy is usually swallowed in tablet form and can come in a range of colours and sizes but is usually white. The user feels fantastic and loses inhibitions about an hour after taking the tablet and the effects last for another four to six hours. If you take it in a club, the advice is to drink a pint of water every hour. At least 60 people have died in Britain after taking Ecstasy. It is a Class A drug.

● **Alkyl nitrates** *(poppers):* This comes as a clear or straw-coloured liquid or as a vapour, breathed in through the mouth or nose from a small bottle or tube, which gives you a brief rush to the head. The effect goes after a few minutes. Possession is not illegal but supply usually is. It is particularly dangerous for anyone with heart or breathing problems.

● **Amphetamines** *(speed, whiz, uppers, amph, Billy, sulphate):* This is a grey or white powder that is snorted, swallowed, smoked, injected or dissolved in a drink. It also comes in tablet form. It is a Class B drug (or Class A if prepared for injection). A new, very dangerous form called metamphetamine (or ice or crank) is beginning to appear, which you can smoke and which retains an intense effect. Amphetamines produce feelings of alertness and stamina. After-effects may include depression, and long-term use may lead to mental illness. You can also die from an overdose.

● **Magic mushrooms** *(mushies):* Mushrooms are eaten raw with food or brewed into a drink. Some mushrooms can cause bad trips. Others are poisonous. It is not illegal to possess mushrooms, but it is illegal to prepare them for use. They are then regarded as a Class A drug. A low dose has similar effects of relaxation to cannabis. A high dose is more like the experience with LSD. A 'trip' lasts about four hours.

DRUG CLASSIFICATION

● **Class A** (heroin, methadone, crack, cocaine, Ecstasy, LSD and amphetamines if prepared for injection)
Conviction for possession can lead to seven years in prison plus a fine.

● **Class B** (amphetamines and barbiturates)
Conviction for possession can lead to five years in prison plus a fine.

● **Class C** (mild amphetamines, anabolic steroids and cannabis)
Conviction for possession can lead to two years in prison and an unlimited fine. Conviction for trafficking can lead to five years in prison.

● **Cannabis and the law** Cannabis was reclassified in 2004 as a Class C drug. It remains an offence to grow cannabis, to own it or to supply it. If you are caught with it, you are most likely to be cautioned or fined, although repeat offenders can be prosecuted and sentenced. Serious suppliers can get up to 14 years in prison and an unlimited fine.

It is dangerous to drive while under the influence of cannabis. The police now have Field Impairment Tests to find drug users on the road.

● **Alcohol** and **nicotine** are also drugs. It is illegal for shopkeepers to sell cigarettes to people under 16. It is illegal for shopkeepers to sell alcohol to people under 18 and illegal for under-18s to buy it. Personally, I can see no merits whatsoever to smoking and considerable downsides to your health and your purse. Alcohol can be dangerous. However, it is at least a legal drug and you get what it says on the label.

● **Legal Highs** Legal Highs are new drugs on the market, which are sold as an alternative to Ecstasy or speed. Brands include Nirvana

Plus, Salvia, Cloud 9 and herbal ecstasy. The law is always play-ing catch-up with drug production and these drugs are not cur-rently illegal under the Misuse of Drugs Act (although some require a licence to be sold under the Medicines Act). However, very little is known about them and very little research has been done. The fact that they are not illegal does not make them safe.

'There are lots of drugs around wherever you go, especially at univer-sity. Mostly it's not been hard drugs. Marijuana and some cocaine, and lots of people popping pills. It's all very available. If you can't do drugs in moderation, you shouldn't do them. It's easy to lose control. I'm not big into that rebellion thing but a lot of people lose control when they come to university, particularly the ones who have had strict par-enting. I know a guy who came from a very strict background who thinks it's great to get drunk every night and takes loads of drugs. It's classic.' ED, 21

'Drugs were more an issue for me at school than university. At uni-versity it wasn't the big taboo thing and there wasn't the peer pres-sure or the shock value. Two boys I lived with took lots of drugs. But it wasn't ever really a problem unless they were stoned all day, which was annoying.' ANNA, 24

'Our student halls get raided on a regular basis.' TIAN, 20

'I work doing club promotion so I get to socialise a lot. You see a lot of cocaine in the VIP lounges of clubs. And weed obviously, every-where. I don't do drugs. It's not a moral thing. I'm just not interested.' ALEXIS, 18

'As for drugs, my information came from the media. However, there is definitely a sense of peer pressure in college in certain groups of drug user. It is also a topic not talked about openly among the students because the college has a very strict regulation against drugs.' ASHLEIGH, 18

'I used to smoke quite a lot of cannabis. But then one night (the night of my university interview) I got really paranoid and wondered if I was going to get schizophrenic. I haven't taken any since then. People here smoke a lot of cannabis.' WILL, 18

www.talktofrank.com for free, confidential drugs advice.
Or call **0800 77 66 00.**
www.ndh.org.uk (the National Drugs Helpline,
Tel: **0800 77 66 00**) provides advice for drug users and
their family and friends 24/7. Advice is also available in several
different languages.

Dear Teenager,
48 HOW TO DRINK RESPONSIBLY

Alcohol is a drug like any other, but it is more socially acceptable than some and it is legal. However, it can still be dangerous and damaging in both the short and long term.

- 40 per cent of cases that go to hospital emergency departments are thought to be alcohol related.

- More than a million alcohol-related crimes are committed each year.

- 17 million working days are lost because of hangovers or alcohol-related illnesses.

- Not only are lots of accidents caused by binge drinking, but heavy alcohol use can lead to long-term illnesses including cirrhosis, ulcers, heart disease and some cancers.

- People are starting to binge drink younger and younger.

- Alcohol and sex can be a bad combination. Young people often say they regret having had sex and only did so because they were drunk. There is a link between alcohol and unsafe sex. Condoms aren't the first thing on your mind when you are tanked up with alcohol.

The government publishes safety guidelines for drinking. The guidelines apply to adults. The recommended maximum is 21 units a week for men and 14 for women. A unit is a small glass of wine or half a pint of beer.

ALCO FACTS

● One alcopop or 1 pint of beer = 180 calories.

● It takes about an hour for the body to get rid of one unit of alcohol.

● The legal driving limit in the UK is 80 mg of alcohol per 100 ml of blood.

● Binge drinking is defined as more than ten units at one session for men and seven for women.

Lots of young people are under the misconception that alcopops (pre-mixed spirits) are safer to drink than other kinds of alcohol. This is not the case. They have a high alcoholic content. Young people say they choose them because they are easy to drink.

The law says children under five may not be given alcohol but otherwise there are no legal restrictions on what age you need to be to drink at home. You can have a drink in a pub or a restaurant while eating a meal in the company of an adult when you are 16 but you can't buy yourself a drink until you are 18.

If you do go out drinking, here's what you need to remember.

● Before you go out, decide what the maximum is that you are going to drink and stick to it.

● Eat before you go out and try to eat when you are drinking. This encourages the absorption of the alcohol. Drink plenty of water.

● Do not indulge in drinking games.

● Switch to a non-alcoholic drink from time to time.

● Make sure you know how you are getting home and do not travel as the passenger of someone who has been drinking, however much they swear they are fine. Naturally, do not ever drink and drive.

'Lots of my mates smoke cannabis and lots drink alcohol. In fact there's a bigger problem with alcohol. People are generally much nicer stoned than drunk. It's not so disruptive.' TIAN, 20

'I don't get drunk. I can't afford to throw away £20. I'd rather spend it on other things.' IAN, 19

'When I was 14 I got paralytically drunk and the emergency services had to be called. The next day, my parents didn't want to talk about it. They told me off, but they didn't discuss alcohol, just me being bad. I think if parents are open, children don't feel the need to prove anything.' KACHENGA, 19

Dear Teenager,
49 HOW TO DEAL WITH A HANGOVER

People who get drunk get hangovers. Alcohol is a drug and drinkers suffer a reaction to too much of it. An excess of alcohol creates a build-up of toxins, which the body has trouble getting rid of. Alcohol is also a diuretic, which means it dehydrates you and gives you a headache. It's a depressant too so the next day it's likely to leave you feeling irritable. Don't forget that driving after a heavy night's drinking can be dangerous as you may well still be intoxicated. If you are in any doubt, don't drive.

So what can you do about a hangover? People swear by their own cures and will come up with lots of fancy recipes that you probably won't feel up to making. But there are certain actions that are likely to help or hinder your progress back to normality.

- Drink water before you go to bed and in the morning. Drink a pint of water for every alcoholic drink you have had.

- A shower may well ease that aching head and massage away some of the pain.

- Coffee isn't the answer. It will wake you up, if that's what you need but it won't help with pain relief and it is a diuretic. And what you need is more water in your system, not less.

- Some people take paracetamol to relieve the headache. Don't take it before you go to bed in anticipation; alcohol does not mix well with other drugs. Leave it until the morning and have it with your orange juice.

- You can drink isotonic drinks, which are designed to replace lost salt and sugars, but they can make you feel bloated because of the gas in them.

- Some people advocate that if you are hung over, you need to drink more alcohol. This is called the 'hair of the dog'. This only gives short-term relief. It may give you a very temporary kick but you'd be much better off drinking a carton of orange juice, which will rehydrate your body.

- Sleep is helpful, as is the passing of time, which is the only real cure. Alcohol spoils your sleep pattern and takes away quality sleep, which of course makes you feel worse. Go back to bed if you can. Hopefully you'll wake up feeling better...

'Hangovers? Oh yes, I've had lots! I drink lots of water and feel sorry for myself and have a shower and start to feel better.' MICHELLE, 19

'I don't like to have hangovers. I do go out and have a few drinks. The trick is to drink as much water as you drink beer. If you have 4 pints of beer, have the same of water when you get home. If you don't, you'll have a stonking headache in the morning.' IAN, 19

'Three cups of green tea and you're sorted.' MATILDA, 20

'Irn Bru! Have one the next morning and you'll be fine.' GEORGE, 20

'The first time I got drunk at university was a hideous experience. I woke to find myself slumped in a hall of residence cubicle with sick all over me. There is no miracle cure. Just drink lots of water before you go to bed.' STEVE, 26

www.thesite.org has excellent advice on alcohol safety and hangovers.

Dear Teenager,
50 HOW TO NOT SMOKE

The law does not restrict smoking to any age but it is illegal to sell cigarettes to anyone under 16.

When my mum was growing up, everyone smoked. It was the cool thing to do. When I was growing up, it wasn't. From the early 1950s the connection had been established between smoking and cancer and it seemed a ridiculous, expensive and self-harming thing to do. Since then much tobacco advertising has been banned and we know much more about the dangers of nicotine. It is ironic then that teenagers today are again taking up the habit fast. More than 80 per cent of smokers start smoking as teenagers. They live to regret it. Seventy per cent of smokers want to give up.

You have to have a bit of a death wish to take up smoking. Smoking narrows the arteries and can lead to heart attacks, strokes or limb amputations. If you are a smoker and use the contraceptive pill you are at greater risk of heart disease. Smokers are more likely to miscarry or to deliver lighter babies. It is thought that there is a link between smoking and impotence. Whenever you are asked to fill out a form for insurance you will be asked whether you are a smoker because it is such a key factor in your health. One in two long-term smokers dies early and loses about 16 years of life.

The trouble is, when you're a teenager, dying aged 60 rather than aged 76 doesn't bother you much. And you've got to die of something, haven't you? Then you are hooked, you have a nasty, killer habit and it's incredibly hard to stop. But did you know that smoking also causes blindness? Smokers are twice as likely to lose their sight in later life as non-smokers. That fact alone should stop you getting started.

It is of course best to not start smoking. But once you have, and you decide to stop, there is help at hand and you can stop.

According to ASH, about 450 children in the UK start smoking every day. About one-fifth of 15 year olds (18 per cent of boys and 26 per cent of girls) are regular smokers, despite the fact that it is illegal to sell cigarettes to children under 16.

● You can go to your GP for help.

● You can contact the anti-smoking organisation ASH, which has lots of advice on its website about the techniques that work and those that may be untested scams.

● You can use nicotine patches, which you stick on your skin like large sticking plasters.

● You can use gum or nasal sprays or lozenges or inhalers. Some people use hypnotherapy or acupuncture (but you should always check that you are using a registered practitioner).

● But most of all you need the will to do it. There are free helplines you can call for advice or support (NHS Smokers' helpline: Tel: 0800 169 0169; Quit helpline: Tel: 0800 00 22 00).

● Any ex-smoker will tell you that giving up is hell to go through, but you will be healthier and wealthier if you can do it. If you smoke 20 a day, it will cost you approximately £2,000 a year. Multiply that by a few years and you may well be shocked by the expenditure.

 www.ash.org.uk is a charity aimed at eliminating the harm caused by tobacco and smoking. It has advice on quitting smoking.

SPEAKING PROPER

TEENAGERS HAVE A REPUTATION FOR GRUNTING. Dunno. Mmm. Later.
Hang on. Whatever. That's forgivable (or rather it's liveable with) while
you are in your teen cocoon and everyone expects you to be a bit
unpleasant and uncommunicative. But the time comes when you have
to emerge, butterfly like, and make an impression on the world. You
don't have to talk posh. You just have to be able to talk coherently and
politely to other people, especially if they are people from whom you
are asking favours. It's not difficult.

A useful ingredient for getting your own way and for getting the best
out of other people is learning to use a dollop of good old-fashioned
charm in all forms of communication, from writing letters to face-to-face
negotiations.

MINI QUIZ

*Test your etiquette. Just how well brought up are
you?*

1. Do you regularly and promptly write thank you
   letters?
2. Have you ever complained about a product and
   achieved the result you wanted?
3. If you are writing a formal letter, is it better to type it
   or handwrite it?

Answers

1. You should have been doing this since you
   were knee high to a grasshopper.
2. Well done if you have. If you haven't, would you
   know how?
3. Type it.

The debating society at school was important to me as a teenager. There was a debate every week. I was shy and loth to stand on my feet but I forced myself to do it and it was really important and a source of confidence ... and a source of terror.

ANTONY GORMLEY, ARTIST

Dear Teenager,
51 HOW TO WRITE PROPER LETTERS

Now that we all use email and mobile phones, the art of letter writing is slowly being forgotten. But there are times when you need to be able to write a good letter.

Thank you letters
Everyone loves to receive a present but very few people are good at sending thank you letters. This is ridiculous. If you don't write a thank you, you don't deserve the present. Looking at it in an entirely self-interested way, you are much more likely to receive more and better presents if you demonstrate your gratitude.

● The secret of a good thank you letter is that it should be personal. There is no point in writing a bland letter that says 'thank you very much for the lovely [whatever]'. That looks as though you simply don't care, and even if you don't care you should look as if you do. Thank the person for the gift. Then go on to describe one other piece of news or reflection. This is the clincher. The letter then stops looking like a duty.

● Thank you letters should be written the day after the gift has been received. So Christmas thank you letters should be written on Boxing Day. Well, you can have a little leeway, but they should be written over the Christmas holidays.

● If you are not a natural letter writer and find the thought daunting, buy a set of attractive postcards and use these so that you are not duty bound to fill a whole sheet of paper.

● Always write thank you letters by hand. Typed letters feel so impersonal.

Sympathy letters

Writing a letter of sympathy about someone who has died is always really difficult. It's very hard to find the right tone. As a result, people often choose not to write. That is a mistake. People are always grateful for letters of sympathy and gain comfort from them. It's important that you overcome your embarrassment and awkwardness and make the effort to write.

● Do not use a commercial card of sympathy, one of those ghastly ones with 'In deepest sympathy' written on the front in gold.

● Write a simple letter in your own handwriting that expresses your sense of loss and concern for the person to whom you are writing. Try to avoid the clichés and write what you feel. Quite often you may be writing to someone you don't know (the mother of your friend, the wife of your teacher). It is good if you can recall something about the quality of the relationship you had with the person who has died. Did they help you when you were small? Did they used to make you laugh? Did they support you in football or share a common passion for jazz? What will their loss mean to you? Think of it as a thank you letter for someone's life. Write it, don't run away from it.

Formal letters

These are the letters you write to your bank manager, your landlord, the person who sold you a dud, or your boss. They need to be business-like.

● If you are writing a formal letter, type it on the computer. Typeface is much easier to read. It also looks as though you mean business.

● Choose a typeface that is clear but does not shout at you. Do not pick a fancy pants curly-wurly style – no one will take you seriously.

● Put your address at the top, and the date. If you are being really proper, you are supposed to write the address of the person to whom you are sending the letter, but I don't think that is necessary. If you have a reference number, use it.

● Use simple, straightforward language. Some people come over all highfaluting and posh when they start to write formally. This is not necessary. Say what you want to say clearly and politely. If you are adding enclosures, say so. If you want them to reply by a certain date, say you look forward to hearing from them by a specified date.

● I think it is appropriate to sign off most formal letters with 'Yours sincerely'. Leave a good space to sign your name and print it underneath. Only use 'Yours faithfully' if you are writing to 'Dear Sir/Madam'.

● Keep a copy of your letter either on paper or electronically and try not to lose it. If the letter is followed by telephone calls, make a note on the letter or in the file of the date, the name of the person to whom you were speaking and what was discussed. Check out **How to Complain** for more tips.

'There's so much formal stuff to deal with. If I needed an overdraft extension, or to sort out my student loan or my housing, I'd have to sort it out myself and it was a bit of a culture shock. The sheer volume of it was shocking. Also, I didn't really pay attention to what was sent me. I kept getting bills for the council tax; I didn't realise I had been sent an exemption form and all I had to do was to send it off.' SOPHIE, 22

'We had the need for thank you letters drummed into us at a very early age and now we're all pretty good and efficient with them. People do seem to appreciate getting them.' NICHOLAS, 15

'I have a general respect for politeness, my family is big on it and I always do thank you's, even for mundane things. If I did something, I think I'd like to be acknowledged for having done it.' ALEXIS, 18

'My parents always encouraged me to write thank you letters. Now I

often send postcards to godparents and family while I'm sitting being bored in lectures. It's a good way of keeping in touch.' WILL, 18

Dear Teenager,
52 HOW TO BE A GOOD GUEST

For most of your early growing up years parents tend to take the lead in where you go and what you do. Your relationship with other adults is very often limited to relatives, teachers at school and other people's parents. Then that all starts to change and you initiate your own social activities. You start having to deal with a wider spectrum of adults, including tutors, bosses and work colleagues.

You need to start exuding a bit of charm. I lived for the best part of a year in Brussels when I was 21. I had a horrible room with no bathroom, just a sink with a dodgy tap and a shared loo down the hallway. My best friend was a Belgian girl whose parents lived in palatial style in the suburbs. They used to invite me for the weekends to their home where I could luxuriate in their good company, their excellent food and wine and their bath. If I had been sullen and grumpy and ignored them or answered monosyllabically because they were adults, I am quite sure that I wouldn't have had nearly so many baths or delicious meals. Adults aren't a different race, they're just older.

To be a good guest you need to show your appreciation. You can do this by saying thank you a lot. You can do it by writing after the event if it's something special. You can do it by taking a small gift when appropriate (nothing showy or extravagant, just something to show you've been thinking of them, such as a bunch of flowers or a bottle of wine). You can do it by engaging with your hosts while you are in their company. Shake hands, have eye contact, smile and add to the conversation rather than making it hard work for them.

If you are staying for a meal or the night, don't expect to be waited on. Lay the table. Clear up afterwards. Ask if you can help. When I was growing up, we had hundreds of lodgers and it was always the ones who helped with the washing up that we liked the best. This wasn't because they were doing a job that needed doing. It was because they were the ones we chatted with and got on with most easily. They were the most relaxed house guests.

If you are in someone else's house, the parents are not your parents. Even if you treat your own mum as a skivvy, that's not appropriate here. You are on new territory. Charm them.

How to be a good guest? Go home soon!

FIONA SHAW, ACTRESS
(AUNT PETUNIA IN THE *HARRY POTTER* FILMS)

Dear Teenager,
53 HOW TO APOLOGISE

Of my three children, there is one who remains in funks much longer than the others. His behaviour isn't any worse. It's just that he digs himself into a deep black hole filled with anger and remorse and he cannot climb out of it. If he learnt to apologise and move on, his life would be a whole lot easier.

We all make mistakes, we all do things wrong. The quicker you own up to it and say you are sorry, the quicker you can get beyond it. There is nothing faster at dissolving another person's anger than an apology that is meant. Showing your remorse makes you vulnerable. ('I made a mistake and they are going to be even madder at me when I 'fess up.') However the person to whom you are apologising will find it really difficult to stay angry when faced with a genuine apology.

Don't leave an apology until tomorrow. Do it now. Let the other person see that you did not want to hurt them and that you regret your action.

Companies are now realising the value of an apology in their customer service departments. (See **How to Write Proper Letters**.) If you deal with a complaint speedily and offer compensation or send the complainant a bunch of flowers or a case of wine and recognise the truth of what they say (you're right, the food did have mould or yes, the flight was delayed for six hours), you undermine their anger and have much healthier public relations. You can have much better parent/teacher/siblings relations by acting the same way.

One last point. I hate it when I hear a parent yelling 'Say you're sorry!' and the child blurts out a quick 'sorry' in turn. That achieves absolutely nothing. It is not a magic word. It only works when given with eye contact and delivered with feeling. That is of course a lot more difficult. Sorry.

'Do I know how to apologise? To my personal tutor, yes, I do. To fellow housemates, maybe. To someone I have no time for, no. I don't think guys apologise as much as girls. Unless it's to girls.' TIAN, 20

'I left home at 16 and I've lived in lots of different places so I feel in a constant state of gratitude to people for putting me up. I don't want to take liberties, so I'm always apologising. I say sorry almost as soon as I meet someone.' KACHENGA, 19

Dear Teenager,
54 HOW TO COMPLAIN

Complaining well is a great and useful talent. My sister has spent many years working in customer service departments and is clear about the clients who get what they want. The ones who make the biggest, loudest trouble get what they want pretty fast because no one can endure the noise and it's not good for company image. So shout if you will. However, I don't recommend it. The person at whom you're shouting is, after all, just doing their job and probably doesn't deserve the grief you're giving them. And you may end up with a headache and high blood pressure. There are better ways...

● The first rule of complaining is to do it as soon as you can. If you are on holiday and the hotel is foul, don't wait until you get home. Tell the manager while you are there. Register your complaint and maybe things can be put right. The same principle applies to restaurants or any other service.

● The second rule is to keep full notes on what you do and what they say and, most importantly of all, whom you are talking to. So if you ring up the council cleansing department, make a note of the name of the person you are speaking with and log the call. When you have to ring back the next week because nothing has happened, you feel a twit if all you can say is that last time you were speaking to a man.

- If you are not happy with the response you are getting by phone, ask to speak to the supervisor. Always try and speak to the organ grinder, not the monkey. Follow up phone calls with letters, typed.

- Even though you are angry, it is usually best to be temperate in your language. You can ask for compensation or replacement goods or an apology without going mad. Think about what you want and be focused on it. Do you just want to tell them how mad and fed up you are, or do you want some action? Or do you want your money back? Concentrate on the outcome.

Some outcomes can take you by surprise. When I wrote a letter of complaint once to Nike on behalf of my son, he received, by return of post, an Arsenal shirt signed by each of the players. This would have been worth less than nothing to a Man U supporter but to him it was gold dust. All his friends asked me to complain on their behalf after that!

'It would have been good to have known how to complain. We had issues with our electricity supplier who we were sure had overcharged us. We wrote them a very bad letter and they told us to shove off. None of us had the balls to ring up and deal with it properly. In the end we paid up rather than get cut off. We did it for a quiet life.' MATILDA, 20

'We had a horrible landlady and we tried complaining about things. She didn't take us seriously. People don't care when students complain. I didn't ever feel particularly confident about complaining about anything. I still don't!' ANNA, 24

'I'm quite bad at complaining. I don't like to make a fuss. I know that sounds feeble. My girlfriend complained at the cinema that the arm of her seat was broken and the manager gave us free tickets, but I'd never do that, I wouldn't want to kick up a fuss.' IAN, 19

'My student loan was messed up and I had to keep going down to the offices to deal with it. I got so fed up I started shouting at the incompetent woman, and they called security and I got thrown out. I was ready to strangle her.' SOPHIE, 22

Dear Teenager,
55 HOW TO NEGOTIATE WITH YOUR PARENTS

There are hundreds of guides out there telling parents how to bring up their children and how to pull the wayward ones, from toddler to teenager, back on to the straight and narrow. The books all assume it is the job of the parents to solve the problem and settle the arguments. They have the wisdom of age and, after all, they are the bosses. That's fine if you want to do it that way, but it is every bit as possible for you to be as manipulative as them and to achieve the results you want. Most jobs and most relationships involve negotiating skills. You might as well start to acquire the know-how now and benefit from it.

● Shouting does not usually do the trick. In that kind of confrontation, everyone feels they need to win and have the last say, especially parents. So, whatever you say, they are likely to top it and to make more venomous threats than they probably want to. You wanted to go to a party tonight and your parents want you to stay at home and study instead. You shout, they shout, you shout some more and they decide to have the last word. 'You're not going out tonight, and you're not going out the rest of the week either. You're grounded. That's final.'

● A better technique on your part would be to sit them down at a quiet moment and tell them you want to discuss the party. Anticipate what their concerns are and have an idea of a concession to make. You'll stay in tomorrow tonight to complete the course work, or you've done it already.

● If the issue is more complicated and involves more people, suggest a family meeting. Bring everyone together to discuss the issue and make sure everyone has their say. Don't shout or interrupt. Listen. Show you are being reasonable. Then do your best to get your own way.

Parents are frequently wrong and frequently jump to inappropriate conclusions. They are also often not half as secure in their judgements as they make out. If you take the initiative and add to that a bit of a charm offensive, you stand a good chance of doing a deal and winning the day.

Negotiating with parents is often hard, especially when you are living at home. You all know each other so well and things can get heated and out of hand more quickly than they would in an office or more formal environment. However, if you can learn your diplomatic skills in the tough framework of home as a teenager, you will be well set up for life. Think how useful it will be when you want to negotiate an increase in your pay...

'If I needed a lift because I was tired, it would be no good just saying to mum "I need a lift". I have to offer her something. That's negotiation. Sometimes I don't shave or wash my hair, so I say, "Will you give me a lift and I'll shave?" Or otherwise she'll say "Wash your hair and I'll take you!" But if I've been away for a while, then she'll do anything!'
TOM, 19

'With size comes power. I'm taller than my mum now. She was trying to get my phone off me. I simply bear-hugged her and moved her out of the room. She said it was assault!!' MICHAEL, 15

I had nine brothers and sisters. I ran away from home once. I'd had an argument with my mum. She was really worried. I was scared. Every night my sisters let me in and I slept at home. My mum thought I was sleeping rough but I was in the next-door bedroom!
BENJAMIN ZEPHANIAH,
POET AND NOVELIST

DEALING WITH THE BIG ISSUES

SOMETIMES THINGS ARE JUST THE WAY THEY ARE and there's little you can do about them. Bad things happen. Life isn't a bed of roses. Sometimes problems seem too big to cope with. That's true all through life, whatever age you are. I'm not convinced that adults are any better at dealing with emotionally difficult territory than children. But if difficult things happen when you're young, it often propels you into being grown up more quickly than you had bargained for.

Issues about sexuality, death and depression can all be taboo subjects. You've got to be brave and say what you need to say. Things rarely get better when they are bottled up.

No mini quiz here. The only question is: are you brave enough to ask for help when you need it?

Dear Teenager,
56 HOW TO TELL YOUR PARENTS YOU ARE GAY

Some gay people never manage to tell their parents they are gay. The celebrated actor Sir Ian McKellen has said it is a matter of great regret to him that he never managed to do so. It means living with an untruth and that is a very hard thing to do. Being gay isn't just a matter of sex but of who you are and keeping that hidden is a great strain.

Homosexuality is still a difficult issue shrouded in myths. Although the laws and society are more tolerant now, it is often not at all easy for people to come out for fear of the reaction. Frankly, most people find it hard discussing sex with their parents at all so the idea of discussing homosexuality is daunting. Parents may well not

> **(!)** If you are heading off to university, it may be a good idea to look through the student union alternative prospectuses to find one with an active gay support group. If you decide to come out, you may find it very useful even if you wait a couple of years before you actually do anything.

have much knowledge of homosexuality so you may also be asking them to cross a divide into the unknown. It is not surprising then that some people wait years before they summon up the courage to tell.

How to tell

How you tell them, and when, depends on your family. Some people feel it is best to say to parents that you have something to discuss with them and suggest a meeting. Others say it is better just to blurt it out when it feels right without the formality of pre-arrangements. Some people tell a sister or brother (often they have known for years) and they do the telling. Have a look at some gay and lesbian websites or speak to the Gay and Lesbian Switchboard to find out about other people's experiences and how they coped with them. They say that the biggest single category of calls they receive is from people coming out. Coming out is often a process rather than a one-off event and people phone frequently for support over the course of time.

Your parents' response

Sometimes parents may already have a suspicion that you're gay. However, sometimes it can be the last thing that would ever occur to them. Either way, it is likely to be a shock to hear the fact spoken out loud. Remember, you may have been planning what to do for ages. They have not had time to prepare their reactions. For many parents it can be a death of expectation; expectation of the kind of life they had envisaged for you and expectation of your having children. In the first instance you are sharing with your parents the burden of knowledge and it is a lot for them to acknowledge, process and respond to. They have brought you up from babyhood and here is this other, unknown side of you.

Parents, of course, all react differently. Some say, 'How do you know? Maybe it's just a phase.' Others agonise about whose 'fault' it is, and what they did wrong in your upbringing. (It is of course nobody's fault but people still tend to look at their children's upbringing to search for possible causes.) Some parents immediately think of AIDS. Others simply find gay sex anathema. Or they may immediately regret the fact that they are less likely to become grandparents.

If you are lucky, once they have had a chance to digest it, parents will be very relieved that you have told them and they will want to be supportive and will be concerned only for your happiness.

Understand that your parents may need a bit of time and space to deal with what you have told them. You could suggest talking about it again in a day or so. They need to get used to the idea to be able to come out in turn to their friends and family. If you are telling your parents, it is because you love them and don't want to hide your life from them. Take strength from that. You are not only dealing with your parents' individual reaction but with all the homophobia that still exists in our society. It may be a very hard thing for you to do but remember that it would be harder to go through life not telling.

When a friend tells you they are gay

If you are being told by a friend that he or she is gay, the best thing you can do is to listen and be supportive. Don't immediately bombard them with questions to which they may not know the answers. Don't treat them any differently from before. A common reaction is to feel the person coming out has been lying about everything. Understand how difficult it is for them to come out and what a privilege it is that they have come out to you.

'I came out to a friend after A levels. It was not a good moment to tell because everyone went their separate ways and nothing happened. A year later I started telling old schoolfriends who were supportive and encouraging. I went home for a weekend and meant to tell, but didn't. Next time I decided to say something straight away and didn't again. I went to dinner with my parents and came back to the house and burst into tears. I said, "Mum, I'm gay and I'm so upset because I didn't know how to tell you." She gave me a big hug and said it was fine. Dad said it was fine, too. It was a huge weight off my mind.' STEVE, 26

www.llgs.org.uk (Tel: 020 7837 7324) for the London Lesbian and Gay Switchboard.
www.thesite.org for advice on coming out and further contacts.

Dear Parents,

Some parents are of course sanguine about news like this. For others it can be hard to bear. But for your child to tell you is an act of courage and an act of love. You may feel hurt, angry, perplexed, frightened and even bereaved. Try to show your son or daughter that you love them and respect them for telling you. You will need time to digest the information. Lots of parents say how helpful it is to talk to other parents who have been in this situation. There are many support groups for families of gay people, up and down the UK. You can find them on the internet or through a lesbian and gay switchboard. Ring them and share how you are feeling. They will be able to help.

There are always some parents who tell their child never to darken their doorstep again. It's a loss for the child. It's a tragic loss for the parents.

Dear Teenager,
57 HOW TO TELL YOUR PARENTS WHO YOU ARE SLEEPING WITH

If you're living at home, the chances are that your parents will know a bit about your love life, if you have one, and that can be embarrassing, difficult, a source of consternation or easy as pie. For the most part, once you are living away from home there will be no need to explain your love life. It's not that there has to be any great secret but part of the joy of living away is learning to be yourself and not being under your parents' protective wing all the time. So you're sleeping with him or her; that's your business. However, when the partner comes home to stay, those boundaries all begin to blur and meeting the parents can feel like a huge obstacle course.

Most parents automatically think their children's partners are not good enough. Some parents also look upon each new arrival as a potential son- or daughter-in-law so the occasion becomes emotionally loaded. You may see them as a friend but your parents may see them as potential sperm-donor or egg-bearer of their grandchild. Your parents have looked after you since you were little and their instinct is quite likely to be protective now.

The biggest hurdle, and probably one that will be hotly debated before you even arrive, is whether you get to share a bed together. You may think it's obvious that you should, given that you sleep together the rest of the time. But this is home. This is your parents' territory and you should do what makes them feel comfortable. There is not an inalienable right to sleep together at all times and your parents may feel, for example, that it is confusing for younger siblings if you share a room under their roof. Accept this and don't push your luck. I know I may sound like your ancient maiden aunt but you don't have to be combative over the question of a couple of nights. You never know, your parents might even decide they like your partner and, if they become a regular fixture, they might relax their ideas over time.

It's best not to do anything that turns a visit into more of a challenge than it might be anyway. Remember that your behaviour probably reverts to that of a teenager as soon as you cross the threshold so you are automatically trying to be two people: your parents' child and the independent away-from-home person forming new relationships by choice. Keep the visit short. Check out the advice in **How to Be a Good Guest**, and remember to show your parents you appreciate them, as well as looking out for your guest.

'I never want to talk to my parents about this stuff. I have got female friends who talk to their parents but most of the blokes say nothing at all'. IAN, 19

'My parents say, "Where would be easiest for him to stay?" and I go, "Oh, he can stay in my room. That would be easiest!"' MATILDA, 20

'Me and my brother don't bother taking anyone home. Until I find someone I want to marry, I don't think I'll bring anyone home to stay.' HANNAH, 20

'At home I would never have a boyfriend over to stay. I'd find it very uncom-fortable and so would my parents. It's more liberating being away.'
ALEXIS, 18

Dear Parents,

Most of the parents I've talked to find this a difficult issue. When a child is living at home it can sometimes be better to let them sleep with a partner under your roof because at least that way you know where they are. On the other hand it implies approval, which you may not feel. If you get through that adolescent obstacle course, or you're lucky enough not to have to face it, the next one is when they are living away but bring a friend home. If you don't feel happy about them sleeping together under your roof, then just say so. It's your roof.

Dear Teenager,
58 HOW TO BREAK UP WITH SOMEBODY

Breaking up is never nice and never easy. I think the most unpleasant phrase in the English language is 'I'm dumping him (or her)'. The phrase evokes everything unpleasant about the situation and suggests a casual cruelty.

Just because you've gone off someone doesn't mean that you have to be horrid. If a relationship isn't going anywhere and you want to finish it, you have two responsibilities. The first is to do something about it and the second is to do it with clarity.

Doing something
- Don't sit around waiting for a right time.
- Don't tell all your mates what you're thinking of doing so that the person you've been going out with is the last to know.
- Don't bottle out and do it by writing or telephone or email. Do it in person.

Doing it with clarity
- It's not helpful to be ambiguous and to hope they get the general idea.
- Don't say you're beginning to think something when in fact you've already decided. Be straight.

Above all, remember it might be you doing the dumping this time but next time the boot might be on the other foot. Just because a relationship has ended and it's not the romance of the century, doesn't mean that people shouldn't be able to walk away from it with their dignity intact.

'Don't do it by text. One of my friends did it by text and it was really harsh.' JOCASTA, 18

I think this should be taught at school. In my day, if you were going out with a boy, you wore his scarf. When it was over, he said, 'Give me my scarf back,' and that was that. It was full of hurt. Breaking up is always awful. FIONA SHAW, ACTRESS

(AUNT PETUNIA IN THE *HARRY POTTER* FILMS)

Dear Teenager,
59 HOW TO GET HELP IF YOU'RE FEELING DESPERATE

There are all kinds of times in life when we need help but don't know quite who to ask. Maybe you don't want to talk to family or friends or teachers. That's when you can use a confidential helpline. They won't laugh at you or think you're silly. They can help you with information, they can lend you an ear and they can offer you support.

Boys are more reluctant to ask for help than girls. They have been programmed to think it is a sign of weakness and often they are not good at talking about their feelings. Given that four times as many young men commit suicide as young women and a quarter of all deaths among young men results from suicide, such reluctance is a sad state of affairs. Calling and asking for help is the first step to making things better. There are several services available, including specialist helplines dealing with particular problems.

ChildLine is a service dedicated to helping children and young people. You can call free at any time and the call you make will not appear on a phone bill. Your call is treated in confidence unless you are in danger.

People call for all kinds of reasons. It may be because they are feeling depressed, being bullied, lonely or perhaps because they have suffered sexual abuse or there is domestic violence at home. More than half a million cases of domestic violence are reported in England and Wales each year and, in nine out of ten of them, there are children in the house. People also call because of much smaller problems. ChildLine says no problem is too big or too small. They will try to help you deal with the problem and, if you want them to, they will talk to people on your behalf.

Another well-known helpline is the **Samaritans**. They know that sometimes it is not enough to talk to friends as they may be too close to you. Or you may worry that your misery is making them feel worse. Or you may simply feel your friends think you're a pain if you keep on pestering them. You need to talk to someone who will listen sympathetically and non-judgementally. That's what Samaritans are for. You can call them 24 hours a day and a trained volunteer will listen to you and offer emotional support. Although Samaritans are best known as a service that people ring when they are feeling suicidal, you don't have to feel suicidal to call. You can call whenever you need to talk to someone. Remember, it's not a sign of weakness to ask for help. It is a sign of strength. In the UK and Republic of Ireland they get five million calls a year and 36,000 emails. They will talk to anyone who calls, whatever their age, but if you are under 16, you might want to try ChildLine first.

Samaritans is a confidential service. They only break confidentiality in a very few and specific circumstances such as if they have been told of a terrorist threat. You can find a list of those exceptions on their website.

 www.childline.org or call **0800 1111**.
www.samaritans.org.uk or call **09457 90 90 90**.

Dear Teenager,
60 HOW TO COPE WHEN SOMEONE DIES

When someone dies, it is always a shock, even when you have been expecting it. There is no easy way to deal with the feelings that you have when it happens and no set pattern to follow. No one can say that you'll feel bad for a week or a month but then after two months or a year it will be OK. Grief follows its own path.

You do need someone's shoulder to cry on. Grief is harder to go through alone. Accept help and recognise that that is a positive thing to do. You may find that, as well as the invaluable support of friends and family, it is helpful to talk to someone with whom you are not emotionally involved. I would recommend Cruse, which is a charity that offers bereavement help. Part of their organisation is dedicated to helping young people cope with the death of their friends or family and they can offer help in lots of ways. They have an excellent website, which uses other people's experiences to show you how they have dealt with their grief (*www.Rd4u.org.uk*; the horrible acronym stands for 'Road for you', meaning everyone has to find their own way of coping with grief).

You can read on the website about people who have lost parents or siblings or friends and see what they felt. You can look up a timeline and see what a person who has lost someone feels like after a week, a month, six months or a year. There is some encouragement to be had from reading about other people who have had feelings like yours. There is also encouragement to be had from knowing that no one feels quite the same way, and that grief is individual.

The site also offers you the possibility of writing to the person you have lost and putting your message on the notice-board. So often we feel that there are things left unsaid. It can be therapeutic to write those feelings down, perhaps as a letter. If you don't want to share it on the notice-board, you can consider burying it with the person who has died, or simply keeping it in a safe place for you to come back to if you want to.

The site also has a gallery where you can place pictures or poems in memory of the person who has died. In the first few weeks when there is much happening with the funeral and all the arrangements, there is a rush of activity and concerned people. Sometimes grief can be harder to deal with when everything has settled down and you are supposed to carry on with life, but feel the gaping hole. Being able to create a small memorial for the person you loved may be a positive and helpful thing to do.

However you feel (and you will have lots of ups and downs, probably for a long time to come), you do need to find a way of sharing those feelings. Bottling it up and just trying to get on with life is not the best way to deal with grief. If you feel very desperate there are always people like the Samaritans (see **How to Get Help if You're Feeling Desperate**), who will talk to you day or night. Take that first step and talk.

I sat and read the messages and stories and tributes on the Rd4u website and howled. There was so much grief and pain and longing. Two thoughts came through most strongly. The first was that grief shapes you as a person. You will carry it with you for ever. The second is that life can get better again.

'When my Grannie died, Mum planted a memorial tree for her. She cut off two leaves, one for my sister and one for me. We wrapped them in paper and I put mine under my pillow. It's been there ever since and it makes me feel close to Grannie.' JOCASTA, 18

www.Rd4u.org.uk (Tel: 0808 808 1677) is the website of the youth involvement project of Cruse, the charity that helps bereaved people. They also have a free and confidential phone helpline.
www.winstonswish (Tel: 0845 20 30 405) offers help for bereaved children and young people up to the age of 18.

FROM A TO B

MOST CHILDREN FROM THE AGE OF ABOUT 11 suddenly discover the joys of independent travel. After that there's no stopping them. I thought Nicholas was turning into a true anorak when he started whizzing round the tube system with his friends, creating races to get to Mornington Crescent and Cockfosters and back quicker than the competition. Then I discovered that my husband has always wanted to go round the entire tube system in a single day. So maybe it's a boy thing.

From discovering public transport, it seems like the blink of an eye before teens start to yearn to drive and then are off and away on holidays, gap years and life away from home. But are you capable of independent travel?

'It's really liberating being able to go by train and bus wherever I want but it doesn't stop mum wanting to know exactly where I am. I can't wait until I'm 17. Then I'm going to drive the car.' NICHOLAS, 15
(No he's not. **Ed**.)

MINI QUIZ

Can you navigate your way round town safely, or are you still begging a lift?

1. How do you get a minicab?
2. What percentage of people fail their driving test?
3. Which group of people has the most traffic accidents?

Answers

1. By phoning for one. You never pick one up on the street.
2. 68 per cent.
3. Men under the age of 25.

Dear Teenager,
61 HOW TO BOOK A CAB

Every month in London alone there are ten sexual assaults in illegal minicabs. Just because you are paying someone to take you home, does not mean that you will be safe. If you flag down a car on the street, or someone says 'Taxi!' and asks if you want a lift, how do you know that they are a bona fide taxi service? Would you just get in the car with anyone? Do you know how to tell the difference between a taxi, a minicab and an illegal tout?

I booked a cab for a friend to go home once. It turned up at my home and she went. Two minutes later, another cab appeared, and this was the proper minicab. I have no idea how it happened but I guess a tout must have intercepted the call somehow, and I spent a very anxious hour before I heard she had arrived home safely. That time we were lucky.

Taxis

A taxi cab has to be licensed and drivers are strictly regulated. They have to have proper car insurance and they are vetted for criminal convictions. Taxis have a licence on the back, which identifies that particular vehicle. Taxis are not a cheap option. They charge using a meter according to how far you travel and the time of day and the fares are determined by the council that awards the licences. They can charge for extras such as luggage. They also charge waiting time, so don't hang about! You can safely hail a taxi on the street.

Minicabs

There are two sorts of minicabs or cars for private hire: licensed and unlicensed. You should always use a licensed cab and you must always book them through a licensed operator. This means never booking directly with the driver and never picking one up on the street. The two types of cab look the same although the kosher one will always display its licence. In some places, licensed cabs carry a sticker saying 'not insured unless pre-booked' as an additional warning. In London you can check if a company is licensed or not on the Transport for London website: *www.tfl.gov.uk*.

When travelling by minicab:

- Never hail a minicab in the street.
- When you book a minicab, always ask what the journey is going to cost.
- When the cab arrives, make sure the driver knows your name and destination. Do not get in the car otherwise.
- Lastly, sit in the back and do up your belt.

Depending on where you live, you may find there are women-only cab companies. You can find them on the net or in the phone book.

Make sure you think about your return journey before you set out. Maybe you could halve the cost of a cab by sharing it with a friend. If you have made a plan beforehand, you won't get freaked out at the end of the evening and pushed into an arrangement you're not comfortable with.

'Students are the only people who can ring and order a minicab when they are totally drunk and still sound sober. It's a must-have survival skill.' TIAN, 20

'My biggest spend is transport. I insist on wearing high-heeled shoes everywhere. I don't understand the bus system here yet, and I can't walk in my shoes so I always get cabs. Loads of money gets wasted doing that. I always get registered cabs and I always keep the telephone numbers on me.' ALEXIS, 18

 www.tfl.gov.uk for latest London travel news and how to contact licensed minicabs.

Dear Teenager,
62 HOW TO DRIVE A CAR

Children always fantasise about driving. I suppose it is the ultimate adult occupation. As a child you treat your parents as taxi drivers wherever possible but the notion of getting behind the wheel is liberating and powerful. The trouble is, it can also be a death wish, particularly if you are a boy. Although Britain has one of the best road safety records in the world, most traffic accidents happen to

> ! New drivers are more likely to have an accident within the first two years of passing the test than at any other time in their driving career. In the first year, one in five new drivers are involved in an accident.

male drivers under the age of 25. If men under 25 were prohibited from driving, the world would be a safer place.

Also, given that carbon monoxide from cars is one of the worst offenders in terms of polluting our environment, it would be brilliant to curb everyone's enthusiasm for cars and take a bike or a bus instead. There's never anywhere to park, and congestion charges cost a fortune. Cars are often important to parents with small children and large amounts of shopping. For most of the rest of us, there are often other alternatives.

If you are determined to drive, and if common sense, the desire to live and finance aren't major issues, then here is the deal.

- To drive a car you need a valid provisional licence and a road-worthy vehicle, which is both taxed and insured. If your mum or dad or someone else is brave enough to want to give you some practice, they need to be over 21 and to have held their licence for at least three years. Their insurance company need to be told that there is going to be a learner behind the wheel. You also need to display an L plate (or a D plate in Wales) on both the front and back of the car.

- The driving test comes in two parts, theory and practice. You can take the theory test once you have a valid provisional licence. For car drivers, the earliest date you can have a provisional licence is your 17th birthday but you can apply for the licence three months beforehand. You cannot book your practical test until you have passed the theory test.

- You can also drive a motorbike or a scooter. The minimum age for a scooter with an engine capacity of less than 50 cc and a maximum speed of 50 mph is 16. You need a provisional licence and to validate it you also need to take the compulsory basic training course as you do for a motorbike.

- Lessons cost between £20 and £30 an hour and the Driving Standards Agency, perhaps conservatively, recommends taking 40–45 hours of paid tuition before a test.

- If you eventually own a car yourself, you will have to take out insurance as well as road tax (see **How to Get Insurance**).

There is one piece of good news for drivers and pedestrians. The driving test was first introduced in 1934. In that year, 7,343 people were killed as a result of road accidents. Today, with 31 million vehicles on the road, the accident figure has nearly halved. I'm rather startled by that statistic; I'm sure I would have guessed the opposite. Perhaps we're better drivers than we think. Perhaps also the driving test is appropriately hard. You will find it very challenging (I've never met anyone who found taking a driving test a doddle) and it will also be very expensive.

As for the bad news; in 1934 the pass-rate was 65 per cent. Now it's fallen to 42 per cent so you could be in for more lessons and more money.

'I had my first driving lesson the day after my 17th birthday. I had 22 lessons. I took my theory test three months in. I took my test exactly six months after my birthday and passed first time. I love driving. Touch wood, I haven't had an accident. You've got to be aware not to drive stupidly fast when you haven't got the road experience. I can see now that two-and-a-half years on I'm a much better driver and I'm glad I didn't try to show off and drive like an idiot when I started. I do know people who wrote their cars off at 17.' IAN, 19

'I drive. I took 25–30 lessons as soon as I was 17. I'd saved up quite a lot and got a car. I was desperate for the independence. I love it, it's brilliant. It's especially good for a girl coming home from places in the middle of the night. My parents are much less worried about me now. I use it all the time when I'm at home although I have a terrible sense of direction!' HANNAH, 20

www.dsa.gov.uk which is the Driving Standards Agency. It has good, clear information about the driving test.
www.dvla.gov.uk for detailed information on getting your driving licence and taxing your vehicle.

Dear Parents,

If your son or daughter persists in learning to drive despite my best endeavours to put them off, you should think about post-test driving courses such as Pass Plus. Pass Plus involves six modules: in town driving, out of town driving, dual carriageway driving, motorway driving, night driving and all-weather driving. It isn't cheap but young drivers who take post-test courses can get large discounts off insurance when they get their own vehicles.

Or, if your son or daughter is employed and is able to claim mileage back from their company, they can try asking for extra training. Twenty road deaths each week and 250 serious injuries are thought to involve people at work so employers are wise to consider the issue.

Dear Teenager,
63 HOW TO BUY A CAR

Buying a car may be the first large purchase you have ever made. The seller can probably see you coming a mile off and is rubbing his hands with glee. If you don't want to be fleeced, take care, take your time and do your research.

● You can buy a car from a garage, a private owner (through a magazine such as *Exchange & Mart*) or even, if you are brave enough, an auction. The safest and most expensive method is the garage. However, if something goes wrong after the sale and the garage has mysteriously disappeared, your rights also disappear. So the safest option is an established garage.

● The more you know about cars, the more you can check yourself, but if you don't know much about what lies beneath the bonnet, you are probably wise to try to rely on some professional help. Inevitably this will also cost you dear. From one of the motoring organisations like AA or RAC you can pay for a history check on the car you want. This determines whether the car has been stolen, written off by an insurance company or there's still money to pay on it.

● You can also pay for a vehicle examination, which means someone who knows what they are doing makes the basic checks on the car. They'll see if it has been re-sprayed to conceal the fact it has been in an accident and will check that the car is structurally sound. You might be happy buying an old banger but you need one that is safe and that goes. If you can't afford a professional check, try and find someone else to look at the car with you.

● Once you have made your decision, you need to agree a deal. Most second-hand sales have room for negotiation. Don't believe the price you first see on the windscreen. You are not buying a fixed-price tin of beans from the supermarket. You need to barter. And to barter you need ammunition.

● Go and buy some car magazines or put 'Car broker' into Google. If you are looking at a specific vehicle you can then look up similar models of a similar age and see what price they are selling for. You can source a vehicle this way or you can take that information to your seller and point out that you could buy an equivalent car up the road for a thousand pounds less. We're not all born negotiators, so take a pile of relevant magazines or printouts with you to help your cause.

● If you are buying from a garage, they are very likely to offer you a finance package. Do not simply sign on the dotted line. Check out first of all what your bank will offer you as a loan. A one-size-fits-all garage deal may not be the one that suits you. When you do sign, make sure to check all the small print.

● Your road tax will probably be included in the sale but you will have to find an insurance deal before you can drive the car away. Again, do your research. Insurance is really expensive for the under-25s so you need to hunt around for the best bargain. It is illegal not to be insured.

● When you're working out the cost of your car, remember to add in your annual service, your repair costs, your road tax, MOT and your insurance. It can make the bus seem like a very cheap option!

'I paid for my car myself. I started working before my GCSEs and I knew I was saving for a car then. I had to save hard to do it but I was determined. I looked through all the internet sites and magazines and when I went to view a car I took my Dad with me. He's bought more cars than I have!' IAN, 19

Dear Teenager,
64 HOW TO LOOK AFTER A BIKE

A bike is a great way of getting round but it does require a minimum of maintenance and the application of common sense in order to keep you safe. It may be incredibly boring of me, but I get really cross seeing adults and children alike on their bikes with no helmets. A doctor said to me that it only takes one stint in A&E to convince a person that helmets on bikes are essential. Cyclists without helmets admitted to hospital with head injuries are 20 times more likely to die than those wearing helmets.

You need to keep your bike in reasonable condition. Real aficionados will have an extensive list of checks for your machine, which involve taking it to pieces regularly and cleaning it with a toothbrush. I can only applaud such meticulous care but work on the basis that most people, more used to taking ballpoint pens to pieces and never being able to put them together again, will be better off aspiring to a more modest care regime.

I went for a basic bicycle maintenance lesson with Daniel at my local shop and these are the things he says you must do.

- Your bike should be kept dry. Either keep it in a shed or the hall or invest in a bike cover that you can sling over the top. These covers have an irritating habit of filling up with rain water, which sloshes over you as you remove them, but they do keep your bike in better nick.

- Your bike should be kept clean. Sadly this doesn't mean spraying with the hosepipe. You should wipe the frame down with a damp cloth (not soap and water my expert says because they attract dust), preferably using a bike cleaning liquid.

- You should lubricate the moving parts, the chain and the pedals with a specialist product, such as GT85, but don't get any lubricant on the brake blocks.

- You should also check that the head-set or stem, which holds the handle bars on, is tight.

- Every time you go out you should check the pressure of the tyres to make sure they are well inflated. Daniel says the tyres should be inflated to just under 40 psi, but I only have a basic pump and simply have to feel the tyres to see that they are hard.

- If you are going to travel in the dark, you must have front and rear lights, but not flashing lights (even though they are available for sale, they are not legal).

- It goes without saying that you need a bicycle lock or you won't own your bike for very long. If you have quick release wheels you either need a lock that includes both wheels or you need to remove one wheel and chain it to the other.

- Use the roads with real care. Give large vehicles plenty of space and never cut inside. Always beware drivers just ahead of you turning left. Somehow drivers seem to find cyclists invisible.

- If you can learn to do your own puncture repairs, that's fantastic. If not, and if you're not a mechanic, book your bike in with someone like Daniel for a professional service at least once a year. You'll have far fewer problems and your bike will have a much longer life.

- You should make a note of the frame number and other details of your bike on the police approved property ownership register at *www.immobilise.com*. This gives you more of a fighting chance of getting the bike back if it has been stolen. (For more details, see **How to Keep Your Mobile Phone Safe.**)

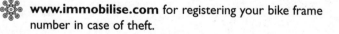 **www.immobilise.com** for registering your bike frame number in case of theft.

DOSH

THERE IS NEVER ENOUGH MONEY, however much you have of it. We all think we'll be happy if we can just get that CD/coat/ jacket/car/house/second house. Frankly, it's just not true. We are never satisfied and we live in a culture where we are persuaded to buy new, bigger and better, and last year's model is so yesterday. The happiest people, in my experience, are the ones who learn not to be envious of what everyone else has. But it's also part of the teenage condition to want to have every piece of latest gadgetry and to behave like the last of the big spenders. Then when you leave home and are paying your own way, it can come as a shock to learn how expensive life is even without all the fun extras.

So if you're going to spend it, you've got to earn it and spend it wisely. You need to know how to budget. You also need to know how to restrain yourself today in order to have something to spend tomorrow.

MINI QUIZ

Are you a spendthrift or the last of the big spenders?

1. At what age legally can you do paid work?
2. If you go to university, how much debt are you likely to come out with?
3. What is a PIN number?

Answers

1. Age 13, for two hours a day on school days.
2. Perhaps you should place a bet on it now. The average student debt in 2005 was £13,500, predicted to rise to £20K within three years.
3. Your PIN number is your personal identification number for your bank card.

163

Dear Teenager,
65 HOW TO USE BANKS AND BANK CARDS

Choosing a bank

Banks know that people often can't be bothered with the hassle of changing to a new bank so they are all very keen to get your custom at 18, knowing they may well have a customer for life. They offer lots of inducements, from free CD holders or DVDs to shopping vouchers or just plain cash. Do not be misled by these offers, which will be gone in a puff of smoke. Think about your overall needs.

You will need a current account with a chequebook and cheque guarantee card. You will want a savings account with decent interest. This is called the APR (annual percentage rate). You will want to have a free overdraft facility so that you are not charged if you go overdrawn. You may want to be able to get a loan from the bank.

You can choose between a high street bank, a building society (they now very often offer similar services to the banks), an online bank (may be cheaper because they don't have to staff high street banks) and an ethical bank (makes ethical or 'green' investments). You will want one that has branches near you and lots of cash machines (see **How to Use Cash Machines**) that are free to use. You may also want a bank with online or telephone banking facilities so that you don't have to spend hours in a queue.

You need to make your choice after comparing what's on offer. These are the people you will be dealing with if you come financially unstuck.

Whichever bank you choose, you will receive a bank statement, usually each month, which details all of your transactions. You should check this because mistakes can be made, and keep it for reference in a financial folder.

Bank cards

There are two types of cards you are likely to come across: debit cards and credit cards. Both make money available to you and are incredibly useful. Both can land you up in debt. When you buy things on a card, it feels a bit like playing with Monopoly money and it can come as a great shock when the bills or your bank statement arrive.

A **debit card** takes money directly from your account and pays it to the retailer then and there. So when you pay your bill in Tesco, it disappears straight from your account. There will usually be a spending limit on the card after which it will not work. In some places you can use the card to get cash-back (that is, money from your account, in cash, now). A debit card also functions as a cheque guarantee card and you will usually be asked for it when you write a cheque.

A **credit card** loans you the money you are paying out. You will be sent a bill each month with the payments that are due. You don't have to pay the whole amount at once, but can pay it in instalments. However, if you fail to pay the minimum required, the interest payments are steep and it is easy to fall into a spiral of debt. Even if you pay part of it, you will be charged interest on the outstanding amount. Some people use their cards as a way of avoiding financial planning. If you're going to be short of cash, it's best to get a proper loan rather than run up spiralling interest charges.

Store cards

Lots of stores now offer their own credit cards and try to tempt you with big discounts on your first purchase. They send you a bill each month and you can clear all or some of the amount owing. However, the APR rate is often very high so it can be an expensive way of borrowing money. If you've got the self-discipline, you can apply for a card, buy something expensive with the discount, then cancel the card straight away. However I have to say my experience of doing this was very unsatisfactory and even though I had cancelled in writing, I continued to receive service charges from the store. After lengthy calls and correspondence I wished I'd never started.

Paying in cheques

A key thing you need to know once you are handling your own finances is that cheques usually take three to five working days (sometimes longer) to clear. This means that when you pay a cheque into your account, the bank first wants to be sure that there is money in the account from which the cheque is being paid. You cannot take the money out and use it until the cheque has been cleared. Nor will your account be credited with the money. This can be a very awkward time lag.

Can I interest you in our in store credit card? 50% off everything you buy today...
Do I look stupid?

Beating the fraudsters

You should always keep your chequebook and your cards separately. Don't just bung them all in the same bag or pocket. A con artist can forge your signature on a stolen cheque and back it up with the cheque guarantee card.

Never give out your PIN number to anyone, even if they say they are from your bank. This applies to requests by phone and the internet. Your bank will never ask you for it.

When you write a cheque, always complete the payee section first. You should never leave a cheque blank because it provides a perfect opportunity for a fraudster to write him or herself a cheque for an unlimited amount.

If you lose a card, act immediately (see **How to Use Cash Machines**) before someone else uses your card. Don't simply wait and hope it will turn up later.

'When you first move away from home, it's easy to spend lots of money. I couldn't believe it when I first looked at my bank statements and thought "Jesus, how have I done this?"' ED, 21

'I didn't know about credit cards and I was shocked at the availability of credit. You don't think about paying it back when so much of it is on offer. Some people blew their student loan in a month. Loads of people maxed out on three credit cards. I know people who have left university who are still paying off credit card bills from their first year. My sister says the first thing you should do when you leave home is buy a shredder for the credit card offers that come through the post.' SOPHIE, 22

'When I was at home, I used to get an allowance. But I didn't have to buy anything except a couple of CDs a month. Now I have to buy everything and I spend furiously. I'm not very good with money.' WILL, 18

'I don't have a credit card. I've had a debit card for ages but I don't think I can be trusted with a credit card. Not until I can look after myself a bit better!' MICHELLE, 19

 www.support4learning.org.uk has very good guidance on choosing a bank and compares what each bank offers.

Dear Teenager,
66 HOW TO USE CASH MACHINES

In order to use a hole-in-the-wall cash machine (sometimes called an ATM), you need a bank account, a debit card and a PIN number. Once you have these you will be able to access money at any hour of the day or night (provided the machine isn't out of order!). The money you spend is taken straight out of your account. You can also use the card to pay directly for other shops and services. Now, with chip and pin technology, you will be asked to tap your PIN number into a machine rather than sign for a transaction.

The bank will inform you of the daily cash limit you can take out. You need to have enough money in your account to cover the withdrawal or have enough within an overdraft facility agreed with the bank.

You don't need to wait until you are 18 to have a cash card (but you do need to have an account). You will only be able to use the card to withdraw cash (if you have any!) but it saves you needing to carry so much cash around with you when you go shopping. You can also use some cash machines to top up your mobile phone.

- To use the machine, you need a PIN number, which the bank will send you under separate cover from your debit card. When you first receive it, you will be given the option of changing it to something you can remember more easily. This number is going to be crucial to you so it does need to be something that comes automatically to mind even if you are exhausted or preoccupied.

- Do not choose obvious serial numbers such as 2, 3, 4, 5. Do not choose recent years. You do not want to make it easy for someone to guess your code.

- You should learn the code by heart. You must not write it down and put it in the back of your purse/wallet or your pocket or your handbag. If you have to write it down at all, write it somewhere at home disguised as something else, such as an extension number.

- When you use a cash machine, look first at who is behind you. Lots of people get robbed as they are retrieving their cash and some robbers are looking to see what code you are tapping in.

Take real care. These machines are brilliantly helpful but you have to be sensible about cash being coughed up into the middle of the high street.

● If you lose your card, you need to act immediately. Until you have informed your card supplier and put a stop on it, you may be liable for anything spent on the card. So if you think you'll just leave it a day or two and see if it turns up at home, you could find yourself facing a hefty bill as someone has phoned distant friends in far-flung countries, splashed out on new clothes and stocked up their wine cellar. From the moment you have reported it missing, you are not liable for more than the first £50.

● You should have a finances file in which you keep a record of your card number and the details the bank will have sent you of whom to call if you lose it.

● Before you use a cash machine, check whether it is going to charge you. Increasingly, machines in or outside shops charge hefty fees for their services. If you're only taking out a few quid, you don't want to be paying the same again for the pleasure.

'I've got a debit card but you've got to watch out. I used an ATM in a pub once and it charged me £1.50 to get a tenner out!' MICHAEL, 15

'I'd never had a cash card before. My parents had never really trusted me with one and anyway I had no need, mum was always around. Going out with one was quite an unusual experience. My mum had told me scary stories and warned me to watch my back, so I was quite cautious. A lot of my friends have had cash cards and think it's quite normal. I got quite excited by the whole process. It was a special event for me.' ALEXIS, 18

Dear Teenager,
67 HOW TO BUDGET

Most people only learn to budget when they run out of money. People who have got loads of money don't have to worry about budgets and the rest of us don't enjoy thinking about it much.

● Keep all your bills and receipts. Put each month's worth inside an envelope. Then you will be able to make a proper check of what you are spending against your predictions, rather than using guesswork. You don't have to be an accountant to stuff some bills into an envelope, so just do it.

● To budget you need to plan. You need to work out what your basic costs are. When you are living away from home these may include fees; rent; electric, gas, water and telephone bills; council tax if you are liable. What is left? Or what is the overspend?

● The next thing you need to do is a cash flow. This means working out when your money is coming in and when it is going out in order to see whether you will have enough.

How to do a cash flow

Have a column for each month. On the left of the page, start with the money you have in the bank. Underneath, write your expenditure for the month. Under that put your income. At the bottom you do a sum. Take away the expenditure from the money in the bank, and add the income. The figure remaining is the money you have left at the end of the month. This figure then moves across to the top of the next month's column, and becomes the next month's money at the start of month.

A cash flow is really useful for estimating how much money you'll have in six months or a year, and for helping you make adjustments to what you spend so that you can remain in credit. Of course it will always be an estimate, but if you keep it updated, you'll find that

CASH FLOW

	Jan	Feb	Mar	Apr
Money at start of month	100	30	20	20
Expenditure	120	60	60	70
Income	50	50	60	80
Money at end of month	30	20	20	30

BUDGETING TIPS

● Buy a clip-board, tie a string round the top and hang it on a visible peg somewhere you can't ignore it. Attach all bills to the clip-board as they come in. Remove them when they are paid.

● Keep your bills in order. Have a ring-binder file in which you put all paid bills. Write the date on which you pay them at the top.

● Write a note of everything you actually spend over a couple of weeks and you'll soon see where your down-falls are and where you can save.

● If you are in a shared house and are sharing the respon-sibility of paying the bills, write a note in the front of the file of who is paying what.

you won't suddenly run out of money when you least expect it.

Also, if you make up a table like the one opposite in a spread-sheet such as Microsoft Excel, then you can make the sums auto-mated, as well as the carrying forward from one column to the next. Then if you change one figure, all the others will change to show you what the impact is going to be.

When you are still at home, you can adopt the same principles and make your own cash flow chart. Your income is your allowance. Your expenditure is what you spend your money on. Work out how much you spend each month on travel, entertainment, books and CDs. If you are saving for something (or arguing the case for an increase in your allowance), you will see how much you need or how long you will have to wait.

If you have never done it before, it is remarkable what clarity a cash flow brings. I speak as someone who hates numbers and who freezes over with fear at anything that looks like a tax return, but there is something very satisfying about the sense of order that this process brings. It is quite calming, even when it forecasts debt. You may well find that you are left with a shortfall. The answer is almost certainly not to start paying bills with your credit card. Your fine cash flow chart will demonstrate that you will only have a mounting problem next month. Look at the **How to Manage Debt** section to see what options you have.

'I was on a gap year before college and that taught me a lot about how to handle a budget. I worked as a secretary for a year and earned some money to buy books and things. The idea of credit is very new to me because we handle everything with cash in my country. I still find everything very expensive in Britain. I read English at university so buying books has consumed most of my budget. Travelling is also very costly. Accommodation is another big factor.' ASHLEIGH, 18

'I need more pocket money in order to learn how to budget. If you're given a pittance it all goes straight away and it doesn't encourage you to budget.' NICHOLAS, 15

'I was taught to keep a budget by my dad. He gave me a ruled notebook and showed me how to keep a column for spending, a column explaining the expenditure and a column for the running total. It was a good life lesson.' STEVE, 26

'My flatmates are all different. One works three or four nights a week at B&Q because he really needs the money. Then he has to stay up all hours to get his college work done. It's tough for him. Another gets £40 a week for shopping plus fuel from his parents. Another worked all through his gap year to get enough money to cope at university.' IAN, 19

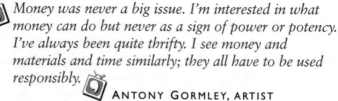

Money was never a big issue. I'm interested in what money can do but never as a sign of power or potency. I've always been quite thrifty. I see money and materials and time similarly; they all have to be used responsibly. ANTONY GORMLEY, ARTIST

 www.studentmoney.org has information on budgeting, including a planner to help you avoid over-spending.

Dear Teenager,
68 HOW TO MANAGE DEBT

So you didn't do a cash flow and you ran out of cash. Now you're in debt and it's hard to know how to get out of it. When you're at school, if you're lucky, being in debt usually means not being able to buy the latest cool gizmo you pine for or not being able to afford to go out for a pizza. When you live away from home, it gets more serious.

I was brought up to think that being in debt was a bad thing and to be avoided at all cost. When I went to university, generous grants were available. Nowadays, with the best financial planning in the world, many young people have to live in debt because there is no other way. So it is not a question of avoiding debt so much as how to manage debt.

10 things to do or not to do when you are in debt
DON'T

1. Don't ignore your bills when they come in. Don't throw away all the brown envelopes that plop through the letterbox. It may be a good idea to pay regular bills with a direct debit (an automatic transfer from the bank) so you don't spend the money.

2. Do not be tempted to take out a store credit card. The APR (annual percentage rate) is usually very high. Most people who take on one of these never intended to do so when they left home. It is not a good thing to make spur-of-the-moment financial decisions. If you have a store credit card, be very careful to check the penalties if you make late repayments. Better still, when you've paid what you owe, cut it up and cancel the agreement.

3. Beware piling up debt on your credit card, horribly tempting as this is. A credit card can be useful in allowing you to delay payment for a month but if your debt accumulates and you are not able to pay it off, the interest rates on these cards are often huge and you can fall into bigger and bigger debt. If you have a card, make sure you clear the balance before the deadline. Avoid having several credit cards.

4. Try to avoid simply slipping into an overdraft. The trouble is, if you go beyond your overdraft limit, the rate you will pay back will be much higher than the one you arranged.

5. Don't panic. It is much better to ask for help. If you are at university there will be financial advisers in the students' union who

will be able to help you. They may also know about any hardship loans that are available. If you are not a student, there are debt advice organisations that can help. Don't get into a spiral of debt in silence. Other people can help you work it out.

DO

1. Review your budget so that you know what's coming in and what's going out.
2. If you are going to university, you will be able to receive a loan from the Student Loan Company. You repay this when you have finished your studies and have started to earn more than £15k a year (2006 figures). Repayments are worked out according to your earnings and are not over a fixed time. The maximum loan is between £5k and £6k. However the loan is very unlikely to pay all your costs. The average student left university in 2005 with £13,500 debt, which increases hugely with variable tuition fees. The National Union of Students calculates that in 2005/6 it cost £10,500 a year to be a student.
3. You can take out a loan from your bank. Make sure you can afford the repayment programme. However, it is usually far cheaper to arrange a bank loan than to spend on a credit card and hope for the best.
4. You can borrow from your parents or discover a legacy from a rich relative...
5. ...or you can get a job. According to the National Union of Students, 55 per cent of students work in term time and, in their second year, 88 per cent work in the summer holidays. Sixty per cent of those questioned in the survey said they had to work to meet their basic living costs. And people who have jobs while they are still at school get very good at handling finances.

'The student loan's pretty good. I've done fine with that. It's excessive drinking that takes quite a lot of people into debt.' HANNAH, 20

'The stereotype of students is that they are so poor that they only eat beans. They're not poor. They spend hundreds on drink and entertainment. They just don't know how to manage money. They are good at getting loans from banks. I've got a friend who got an overdraft on an overdraft on an overdraft.' TIAN, 20

'You need to learn to leech off your parents. Go for a weak point and exploit

it! *"Oops, I forgot my wallet" is always a good line.'* MICHAEL, 15

'Managing a budget has been atrocious. The first term I was so worried I underspent. I scrimped on food. The next term I went in completely the other direction and overspent massively. I had cheques bouncing everywhere. Hopefully next term I'll find a middle way.' ALEXIS, 18

'I work in a night club and in the student bar. I get a student loan of £3k, but that barely covers accommodation, let alone tuition fees and living costs, so I live on a student loan and an overdraft. It will bother me later when I'm paying it back but it doesn't bother me to run it up now. I think of it as me owing my future self some money.' GEORGE, 20

www.adviceguide.org.uk (website of the Citizens Advice Bureau) for financial or legal advice.
www.cccs.co.uk (Consumer Credit Counselling Service) is a debt advice charity.

National Debtline (Tel: 0808 808 4000) offers a confidential helpline plus useful debt advice.

Dear Teenager,
69 HOW TO EARN MONEY

When I was a teenager I used to make a fortune from babysitting. I stayed over at people's houses, went to bed by 10 p.m. and slipped off home the next morning several pounds the richer. If that was work, I was happy to do lots of it. From the age of 16, I got myself a proper job. I was a dental nurse on Saturdays. I found it hard to keep ginger biscuit crumbs, which the dentist liked with his coffee, out of the amalgam mixture for the patients' teeth. I'm not sure how much of an asset I was to the surgery, but it was an entertaining way of boosting my bank balance. Now my 15-year-old son Nick says he wants a job and I think I should encourage his entrepreneurial spirit (whilst keeping him away from the dental surgery I attend), even though I'm sure he ought to be concentrating on the never-ending series of deadlines for his GCSE course work.

Most teenagers are dissatisfied with the allowance that they get from their parents and most parents feel they are being fleeced. Often the answer is to try to earn some money of your own.

Two-thirds of teenagers work at some point. It's hard to calculate the numbers exactly because although employers are supposed to register children working with them, they often don't. There are rules that govern the employment of children and you should be aware of them.

The law says a child cannot be employed:
● under the age of 13
● during school hours
● before 7 a.m. or after 7 p.m.
● for more than two hours on any school day, only one of which can be before school
● for more than eight hours on a Saturday or during school holidays (five hours for children under 15)
● in any job in which they are likely to suffer an injury from lifting, carrying or moving heavy items
● for more than 20 hours a week in school holidays for 13 and 14 year olds
● for more than 30 hours a week in school holidays for 15 and 16 year olds.

The law also prohibits children from working in the following places:
● in a commercial kitchen collecting refuse
● selling door to door without adult supervision
● in telephone sales
● in a butcher's shop or abattoir
● in fairgrounds or amusement arcades
● in any external work 3 metres above or below ground.

That all still leaves plenty of room for manoeuvre. You could think about working as a porter at your local hospital, stacking shelves in the supermarket or bookshop or working at a local café. Or joining a choir and getting paid for singing at weddings if you have a musical bent. Or advertising as a babysitter or dog walker. These sorts of services work best when they are very local and people know you. You can go very, very local and suggest, if you have younger siblings, paid babysitting services at home, but you'd certainly have to offer a special rate.

The danger of paid work is that it interferes with school work and that you fail to get the homework in on time or fall asleep at your desk. It does require real organisation to fit everything in.

Some experts believe it is really advantageous for children to take on a job, not just for the financial independence it gives them but for everything else that comes with the package. In almost any job you're likely to have to be sociable with adults. It can be good for your self-esteem. It might well be good for your CV. And if you go to college and really need to work for extra cash to bring down that overdraft, you're in a much better position to do it then than if you have never worked before. If you find yourself in debt, you may be better equipped psychologically to be able to dig yourself out of it because you know you can earn.

'I'm going to start a job next term. There are loads of jobs around here for students, especially bar work. I do think you have to be careful not to take on too much; maybe not more than two shifts a week. You know you'll be going out on other nights and getting up early for lectures and you can get worn out.' ED, 21

'I've always had jobs and I've always been used to controlling my own money. You have to do a delicate balancing act. You mustn't do too much paid work. You can't use it as an excuse and say you haven't done your academic work because of it. You do get pressurised by your employer to take on more and more.' IAN, 19

'I've always had jobs. When I was at school I was earning about a hundred pounds a week and money was never a problem. I always had enough. When you move out, the first few months you don't quite appreciate how much things cost and you can quickly get into debt: I had no idea how much food costs. You have to learn how to budget.' OLLIE, 18

'It's more satisfying spending money knowing that I've earned it. I get £50 each Saturday. All my friends are jealous. I've struck lucky. Most of them earn half what I do.' JESSICA, 17

Dear Teenager,
70 HOW TO BUY AND SELL ON eBAY

eBay was the invention of a Californian called Pierre Omidyar. He and his wife started up an online auction site in 1995, which grew into eBay, the massively successful global online market-place. So long as you are over 18, you can buy almost anything on eBay from a Cadillac to a Christmas vegetable. You need to keep your wits about you so that you are not fleeced and don't end up buying a turnip.

Selling

Sellers on eBay pay a percentage of the sale price as a fee. When you are selling anything, with or without the internet, you need to operate professionally and truthfully. You have responsibilities towards your buyer. eBay regulates those responsibilities with a code of practice and a safety centre to which you can report difficulties. If you are a seller, you need to be clear and truthful about your product. You need to offer clarity about payment methods. Will you accept credit cards? Will you accept PayPal (as recommended by eBay) or any other third-party payment method? You need to be ready to dispatch the item within the time-frame you have advertised. And you need to decide on a returns policy.

When you are framing your advert, you need to pay as much attention as you would to placing any other ad. After all, you are trying to sell something. It needs to contain all the relevant information and it needs to be placed in the correct category so that it can be found. It also needs to use search-engine-friendly phrasing in its title. This takes practice and research. People scroll through and stop at the interesting titles. A picture is a very good sales aid. Just as with small ads, you can pay for your ad to be given greater prominence.

You need to be available to answer would-be buyers' queries by email. If you don't give sufficient information you will spend a lot of time answering questions like 'How many buttons are there on the flies?' Tell them everything you can think of upfront so they don't pester you.

You can either sell by auction or by fixed price, known as 'Buy It Now'. The auction is timed (from one day to ten days).

You need to be very conscious from your first sale of gathering good seller reviews. This is the key to success on eBay. When someone buys an item, they are asked to report on how the sale worked. Was the item as specified? Did it arrive when promised? This review and rating is permanent and is used as a valuable resource by potential future buyers.

Buying

First you need to register with eBay. You can search for goods by looking in one of a diverse range of classifications (for example, digital cameras) or by being specific about the item you are looking for (a particular brand of camera, new not used). Obviously you cannot see or handle the specific item (but neither can you at Argos) so you need to read the information very carefully. If the item is being auctioned, you can see what the bids are and how long there is to go. Before you place a bid (or the fixed price), check the payment requirements. Some people prefer to use a method such as PayPal, which offers greater security because you are not required to give any card details to the seller and it pays out if you fail to receive the item. However, PayPal does not necessarily cover all your losses. Read the small print relating to the type of item you are buying, especially if you are committing a lot of money. Then check the delivery costs and the returns policy. Finally, and most importantly, read all the customer feedback. Ignore it at your peril.

When you are ready to make a bid, eBay will ask you how much you are prepared to pay. They will then do 'proxy bidding' for you, making automatic bids up to your stated maximum. Once you click to place a bid (or fixed-price sale), you are making a commitment. If your bid is successful, you cannot then change your mind.

People do occasionally get conned on eBay and even with PayPal and the safety centre, they don't always get their money back. At a high street store it is easier to feel confident that you can return goods and complain to the manager. But 25 million goods are available on eBay each day and millions of deals are done and bargains made. Use your common sense. Don't give out personal details, check and double check, and if you smell something fishy, don't buy.

 www.ebay.co.uk – the site offers audio tours and tutorials on buying and selling.

Dear Teenager,
71 HOW TO FIND CUT-PRICE ENTERTAINMENT

They say the best things in life are free, but frankly it can be very hard to find good things to do when you are hard up. I find as soon as I leave the house I start to spend money and my purse seems to haemorrhage when the kids go out. So what can you do for a bit of cut-price entertainment?

● If you're over 16, find out if there is a court room with a visitors' gallery in your locality. Some cases are very gruelling, others are very dull, but it's a fascinating insight into human life and the judicial process.

● See if there is a hairdressing or beauty school near you. My mum goes to a beauty school for cut-price treatments by trainee beauticians. She has massages, facials and other beauty treatments. You can usually get very cheap haircuts too from hair salons that train students.

● Join a team: hockey, football, netball, whatever. You'll have joining fees and subs to pay, but you'll have a lot of fun and a lot of cheap entertainment. Or see if a generous relative will buy you membership of the tennis club.

● Go to a market: craft market, farmers' market or country fair. You can watch craftspeople, see entertainers, watch the horses, taste delicious tidbits of food on offer and soak up the atmosphere. Seal your purse or wallet so you won't be tempted to buy that bargain.

● Check out the websites of TV and radio companies to see if they are recording your favourite programme. Being in a studio audience is great fun and free entertainment.

● I know many people spend their lives avoiding museum visits, but surprise yourself and go to a museum or gallery. They are mostly free entry now and you might find that when you go of your own accord rather than on a school trip or with your parents, you have a very different experience. They also frequently have free lectures

BARGAIN BASEMENTS

● If you are a student, check out the deals you can get with a student card. These cover everything from train travel to insurance to restaurant meals.

● If you are going on a train journey and know when you are going, book it in advance. You will get big reductions if you can buy tickets weeks ahead. Also, if you leave it until the last minute, the allocation of cheaper seats will have gone. Check out coach fares too.

● If you shop regularly in the same supermarket, collect their customer loyalty points and treat yourself when you cash them in.

● Check out the **How to Shop for Food** section.

or other events. They are great places to spend time, to meet people and to see interesting things. They are also good places to use the loo when you're out. Think how cultured you could become after a brief pit stop!

● If you are over 18, check out your local adult education institute. They offer an amazing range of courses for very good value and you could surprise yourself by learning something new.

● Go for a walk. It will do you the world of good and put you in a much better frame of mind than if you stay home and watch the telly.

● Teach yourself to cook. It's not rocket science; you can do it.

The trouble with teenagers is that they always say no to everything and they can't be bothered to do things. It's all too much trouble and not nearly cool enough. I think it's a measure of your maturity if you can get beyond that and recognise that staying at home picking your spots is a lot less entertaining than going out and making things happen. Later on, when you have the yacht and the three houses and the sports car, you can get picky about where you want to go. For now, believe that the world is your oyster, and get out there and make the most of it.

'There are so many leaflets with cheap deals given to students. People target you outside halls. There are deals for everything: drink, food, hairdressing. It's easy to fall into a trap. You go to a cheap deals place and end up spending loads of money. You go on spending more because it's cheap. It's easy to spend money as a student and your parents aren't there to monitor what you spend.' ED, 21

'You really start to appreciate the nice weather when you can go to a park for a kick about with a ball. When you're working constantly and you've got no money, you start to appreciate simple things like that a lot more.' OLLIE, 18

MAKING THE GRADE

LIFE FOR TEENAGERS SEEMS TO BE MORE STRESSFUL THAN IT was for my generation. You have endless exams. You have phenomenal peer pressure. You are expected to achieve. You are sexually mature ages earlier and you are likely to be mired in debt. Maybe all youth today should be required to do yoga (oh no, another pressure!).

You need to keep your wits about you and realise that the whole world doesn't turn on tomorrow's exam or next week's interview even though parents can sometimes make it feel that way. You can also maximize your chances of things going well and maintaining your sanity with sensible planning and a few coping strategies.

MINI QUIZ

Are you in control or are you a loose cannon?

1. Do you always get everything ready the night before?
2. Do you plan your revision or do you just pretend you do?
3. Are you impressed by your own CV?

Answers

1. Top of the class if you are sensible and organised enough to know the benefits of planning ahead.
2. Congratulations if you are a planner. A black mark if you fill in a revision timetable and file it in the bin.
3. Well, if you aren't, nobody else will be. Improve it!

I was a fairly terrified and unconfident teenager. I was no good at sport but I was good at caving and going into holes deeper than other people. I was good at making things ... a sewing basket for mum, a table, a chair, two canoes and a lot of pots.

Art was absolutely essential to me. It's an essential part of schooling because it is the only subject which comes from the pupil. People took me seriously through my art. They would say, 'What is it? Is it finished?' The questions were addressed to me and I was the only authority. I had to take complete responsibility.

ANTONY GORMLEY, ARTIST

Dear Teenager,

72 HOW TO PREPARE THE NIGHT BEFORE

Preparation is anathema to children of all ages. There's no immediate pay-off to it, it's boring to do, and what's the point?

This is one skill that will set you up for life if you can just master it now. Once it becomes second nature, it becomes pain free and brings untold benefits. This very morning Nick missed his bus for school because the trainers he needed for PE were covered in mud and he knew he wouldn't be allowed in the school hall. So we had to attack them with a knife and soak them in hot water. An hour later, when he had PE, they would still have been profoundly damp and unpleasant to wear. He should have had them ready last night.

Each evening do a quick check of what is happening the next day. Do you have your travel pass/money/gym kit/homework/essay/cookery ingredients/clothes? Is your bag packed for the next day?

You should time yourself doing it. It probably takes no longer than 30 seconds. Then, the next morning, when you wake up late because the alarm hasn't gone off, you won't be thrown into a panic because you can't find your keys or your papers. It makes life a lot more pleasant. It stops adults shouting at you. And when you encounter work deadlines in the future, you'll be regarded as ultra-efficient and cool in a crisis.

'Uni has changed me. Before, I was always putting things off until the last minute. Now I can't afford to do that. I get things ready the night before. You have to take on the role your parents have done for you for the last 18 years or so. Up until now you've been spoon-fed.' OLLIE, 18

'I'm not a last-minute person. I do everything in advance. I've always packed my bags the night before. My parents always made me do that for school.' ALEXIS, 18

'You get so much more freedom at university. I expected there to be someone to say, these are the classes you are to go to, these are your deadlines. But there was none of that. You had to go and find out everything for yourself. There's not even an attendance register at lectures. It's your choice. People who hadn't had a gap year tended to say, "What no register? No need to go."' SOPHIE, 22

'What? Prepare the night before? I've never heard of it.' MICHAEL, 15

Dear Teenager,
73 HOW TO COPE WITH EXAM STRESS

Your parents will usually tell you that you've only got one chance and it's your life, and you're crazy if you mess it up now. If you want a good job you need qualifications, so get your finger out and start working properly now. I've been known to say something like it myself. It's not true. There are plenty of people who have got by very well without more than a handful of lacklustre GCSEs. Entrepreneurs Richard Branson and Alan Sugar didn't get degrees. Neither did successful authors P.D. James and Ruth Rendell or Adrian Mole's creator, Sue Townsend. Neither did prime ministers John Major or Jim Callaghan.

You can also re-sit exams, so there is a second chance. These days, the way many courses are structured, if you don't get a good enough grade the first time round, you can sit the exam again and use whichever mark is the better of the two. Nobody ever asks you in later life how many times you sat a particular exam.

Schools and colleges get measured in league tables according to their exam results. This puts pressure on them and on the whole education system to perform. This can be positive; it is in the school's best interest to get you that grade you want. It can also be negative. School feels like an endless exam process with relentless testing, testing, testing every year. This is a real shame because school is about so much else and mugging up for exams is the least interesting part. When I was in my mid-20s and working, I used to have nightmares that I was taking a Greek exam the next morning and I couldn't remember a word of Greek. Clearly exams had got to me.

To keep your cool, you need to keep exams in perspective. They are a very small part of life. They are useful to pass and it's always more fun to do better than to do badly but they are a measure of your performance in a particular subject (and of the teaching of that subject). They are not a measure of the worth of you.

● If you want to relieve exam stress you need to make sure the basics are right. Eat properly. Eating the right food increases your brain power. Sleep for long enough. Sleep can make everything seem a lot better. Take exercise. Not only does exercise make your whole body feel much better, but biological studies now indicate that working out probably benefits the brain too. A bit of oxygen to the brain certainly refreshes that revision dullness.

● Plan your revision and approach it in manageable chunks. Make yourself a timetable and tick off bits as you do them. Put information on cue cards if that helps you or use the revision sites available on the net if you prefer that approach. Do whatever suits you, but break down what you have to do into achievable parts. If you work your way through it methodically, you will have less reason to panic.

● You can't learn everything so try to work out the bigger picture and decide on a strategy. Which question areas are most likely to come up? Concentrate on making sure they are covered. Don't leave looking at your weakest subject until the night before the exam. Break it down into chunks and have a go at them when you're feeling awake.

● It's hard to work in noise and chaos. Find a quiet place to work if you can and organise your revision system so that you know where to find things, whether it is in files or on postcards on the wall or in a card index on your desk. I think there is a little of the librarian in me, and I find it very satisfying to have revision cards all lined up, although I personally draw the line at colour co-ordination.

● Do your best not to get wound up by other people panicking, including your well-meaning parents. And remember that one day you will wake up and be able to say to yourself, 'I am never going to take another exam in my life.' But you might want to wait until you have learnt to drive before you say that.

'The worst thing to do, and I did this a couple of times, is to give only 70 per cent. Then when I didn't do all that well I thought, "Why didn't I just give 100 per cent?" It's better to do your best and to revise hard. On the other hand you have to remember it's not life or death, it's just exams. There's no need to get really stressed.' TOM, 19

'Chill out. I went to sleep in my end-of-year maths exam. That was the ultimate in relaxing. I got 27 per cent.' MICHAEL, 15

Dear Teenager,
74 HOW TO PASS EXAMS

So you've done the revision, or as much of it as is going to happen now. Time's up. It's the exam tomorrow, with endless more of them over the coming weeks. You're sure you're going to flunk the exams, you can't remember anything and you want to emigrate, now.

● Relax. Take a shower. Get an early night. Set the alarm so you're not going to be late. Make sure you've got pens and pencils ready for the exam. Sleep.

● The key step towards passing an exam is to turn up for it on time. I was once having a bath at home when I should have been in the school hall sitting an exam. Exam timetables are ever more complicated. Pin your exam timetable to the wall and always double check.

● I quite liked the challenge of exams. Once you master the technique of doing them, they become more like games and less like torture. I did find one thing quite hard to learn and indeed learnt it the hard way. I took an exam in which I was positive I had done rather well. I did very badly. My essays were great: polished, informed and well structured. But when the exam paper was returned to me, the teacher had scribbled across the front page, 'Read the question!!' I had written excellent essays, which didn't bear much relationship to what I had been asked. You don't get marks for being clever, only for answering the questions.

● Think like an examiner. They want to give you the marks. If you have four essays to write in two hours, spend no more than 25 minutes on each essay (with checking time at the end). Do not spend over an hour on one essay if the examiner can only allocate 25 per cent of the total marks to it. Wear a watch and use it.

● If a question asks for three reasons and there are three points to be awarded, don't quarrel with the examiner and give them two or four. Give them three reasons and pick up the three marks.

● If the exam is handwritten it is always a good idea to write clearly. The examiner should not have to feel he or she requires the skills to decipher the Rosetta stone in order to read your paper.

● Stay calm. You may think the question you are desperate to answer is not there and that you haven't revised for the others. If that's the case, you just have to make the best of it, as if you are playing cards and have been dealt a mediocre hand. You can still play a winning game. And more than likely the question is there but not in the form you expected.

Post-exam analysis syndrome
When it's all over and pens have been put down and you stagger out of the hall feeling as if you have repetitive strain injury in your wrist, do not indulge in a massive, public dissection of the exam. There is no merit in listening to one person saying theatrically that they did terribly, or another wanting to check the answers to the third question and making you think you got it all wrong. Why undermine yourself? What's the point? Better to go and get

something to eat and watch the telly. If you have taken a public examination, you are likely to have to wait months for the results. It is nerve-wracking enough without endlessly replaying and reviewing your answers in your head.

I did not always have this degree of common sense regarding exams. I once took an exam in Greek vases. I was the only person taking the exam. On my examination paper was a picture of a Greek vase. My job was to identify it, date it and determine who the artist was. I really had no idea and had to guess it all. I left the exam, taking the paper with me. As soon as I stepped outside, the picture fell off the paper. It was a postcard, glued on, and printed clearly on the reverse were the name of the artist and the date the vase had been made. I felt really stupid. Not only had I got the answer wrong, I hadn't had the sense to realise that the answer was on the back. It may have been technically cheating to have looked at the back but if I had done so I would have felt less of an idiot (and not just about Greek vases).

Results time

You need to manage the expectations of your parents when you tell them your results. Remember, they are probably more on edge about them than you are. Tell them you did OK in your exam, or not too badly, rather than simply announcing that you've got your results. Then they won't be waiting to hear that you got an A* or an F. (I was quite impressed when I heard of someone getting a U. Apparently this means unclassified. The paper was so bad the examiner didn't even grade it!)

Nicholas told me he had got his French result. I waited for him to tell me how well he had done. '36 per cent,' he said. 'Why so bad?' I asked him, unable to hide my disappointment. 'Oh, it was a really good result. I was only there for 20 minutes. I left early to go to a cricket match, which we won.' I couldn't really argue with that.

'There's a way of passing exams, a few hoops to jump through whatever the subject. Be clear, know a few quotes, and don't get anything wrong!' GEORGE, 20

'You do actually have to revise. There, that's my dynamite advice.' MICHAEL, 15

Dear Parents,

I don't hold with rewarding good exam results. I had friends who were promised £20 or £50 for every A grade they achieved and corresponding amounts for lesser grades. Some people are born cleverer than others and I don't see why luck in the genes department should be rewarded. There are plenty of other things you can give rewards for ... revising sensibly, handling the exam period well, being praised by the history department. I don't believe people perform better in an exam for the sake of a few extra quid. But maybe those people who get given a sports car when they get three A grades think differently, and it's all jealousy on my part!

Dear Teenager,
75 HOW TO PREPARE FOR AN INTERVIEW

Interviews are always nerve-wracking, whether for university or a job. It's a bit like stage fright. If you're not a bit nervous, you can't do it justice. However the last thing you want is to be in a state of panic because you are unprepared. You need to start doing your thinking well ahead.

When you go for an interview, make sure you know about the people you are seeing. There is nothing less attractive than people turning up without a clue. If you don't care enough, why should they bother to take you on? So if you are applying for a job in a wine bar, check the place out and ask friends about it. If it's a chain, look up their website. If you are applying for a placement in a company, for goodness' sake find out who they are so that you are well informed. If you want them to take you seriously, be serious about them. I have interviewed numerous people who want to work in television who appear never to watch any. That doesn't inspire confidence.

● Read job ads with care. Think about the questions they are likely to ask you and consider how to answer them. They are bound to ask you why you want the job, and what sort of experience you bring to it. Think about what they are likely to be looking for and think about what corresponding experience or ideas you can bring. They are not out to trick you, they are out to find someone who fits the bill. Have you got any experience of customer care? Perhaps you have been on the receiving end of it and can talk about how you responded.

- Ask someone to do a mock interview with you so you can practise your answers out loud.

- You may be asked about your strength and weaknesses. Don't think you are in the confessional and have to declare all your shortcomings. Be positive about the strengths and if you conjure up a weakness make sure it is from some time back and has since been addressed.

- You may be asked about a difficult situation. For example, what would you do if a customer swore at you? What would be a sensible response? 'Swear back' would probably not get you the job. Put yourself through this mental obstacle course in advance of the interview and you will be better prepared. And never go into an interview without having one question in your back pocket to ask them. They invariably say 'Have you got anything to ask us?' and if you can only say 'Nothing,' it's a bit of a low point on which to leave the interview.

- Think about what you are going to wear. Obviously certain situations may require certain dress codes. For the most part, my advice would be not to be too formal but to go for casual smart. If you stick on your glad rags that you wear for weddings and funerals, you will probably feel very uncomfortable. Equally I can remember a co-interviewer commenting that she thought someone wasn't very interested in the job because they were wearing their old jeans, whereas she, the interviewer, had troubled to put a skirt on.

- Check the address you are heading for and work out the transport details and how long to leave to get there with a bit of time to spare. You don't want to turn up late, in a flap, blaming the trains.

- When you go in there, walk like a film star. First impressions count for a lot, so make your approach with confidence. Make eye contact with your interviewers, shake hands with them, sit down and keep that eye contact. Try not to be overawed by your surroundings.

- If you are applying for university, do your research about the college and the course just as you should for a job and be clear about your motivations for wanting to go there.

- Often interviewers pack in a tight schedule of interviewees. If you are seeing 10 or 12 people in a day, it can be quite hard to remember who was who (and even whom you liked) by the end of it. It all goes into a blur. Try to engage with them, smile and leave a positive impression. Then go home and relax and forget about it.

'My tip? Just remember, never ever be yourself. It just doesn't work.'
NICHOLAS, 15

Last week I went to talk to 300 six-to-eight year olds and I said to them, you've got to realise that if you really, really want to do something, people will help you to do it. People will be energised by your enthusiasm. Life follows energy, not conformism. People will help you if you are clear enough about what you want to do. ANTONY GORMLEY, ARTIST

Dear Teenager,
76 HOW TO FIND A GOOD WORK EXPERIENCE PLACEMENT

For two weeks, all children in state schools in year 10 and all those from private schools in year 10 or 11 exchange their school desks for the world of adult work. For most children it is their first experience of what adults do all day, other than their teachers.

Some people are cynical about work experience. They say it is just two weeks out of school for teenagers. Parents sometimes see it as teachers taking an extra break. Other cynics view it as cheap labour for the employers who offer the placements.

All of those things may be true sometimes, but it can also be a fantastic experience. It depends a bit on luck and a bit on what you put into it. I have heard stories of shopkeepers who have given students a horrid time and abused them with long hours and too few breaks. School, to those students, has seemed like the better option! I also know others who have had an amazing time and have been very influenced by the experience.

Popular placements include anything to do with the media, which is regarded as trendy. I've given people placements in television companies and it can be fun having an involvement with programmes that you have seen on screen. But you might still find yourself doing grunge work, perhaps logging tapes on to a computer or putting covers on cassettes for hours or playing messenger. You need to be careful with your choice because you might find yourself somewhere that sounds incredibly exciting but in fact you're left to your own devices in a back office and you learn nothing.

Some clever people manage to co-ordinate their placement with their career trajectory. They want to be a lawyer, so they get a placement in a law firm. They want to be a vet, so they get a placement helping at the local animal sanctuary. Work experience can be as useful for demonstrating what you don't want to do. If you don't like the people or the atmosphere somewhere, you may well decide it's the last thing on earth you want to do.

Some organisations are getting more professional about the way they think about placements and they see them as an early recruitment drive. The police, in some regions, offer a week of activities for work placement students and usually try to stay in contact with students who display an interest in policing as a career.

Work experience can also be a useful resource for finding a Saturday job. If you have a good time and do well on a placement, the organisation is going to think much more warmly about the idea of taking you on, on a more regular, paid basis. They already know that in you they have a real gem.

There is no doubt that offering placements is hard work for employers. Most jobs require some form of training and that takes time and effort. Sometimes students think they will easily get a placement in a shop and are surprised to find they are not wanted.

If you are only going to be around for a fortnight, it is hardly worth the store's while to teach you how to use the tills or how to read all the stacking codes, which might take them three days to teach and for you to master.

Think about where you might like to go as early as you can. Inevitably, if you apply late, placements will have been taken. Schools will find you somewhere, but then you will not have much choice in the matter. Use any contacts you can (family and friends), but explore what it is you might be doing on a placement.

There are some rules about work placements and some things to think about.

- You cannot usually work with one person alone. This is obviously for your security.
- The employers have to have a Certificate of Employer's Liability. They also have to be inspected to check they meet health and safety criteria for placements.
- Some companies do not like 15 year olds on placements. They prefer people to come a year later.
- Think about the commute. If it's going to kill you to get there, it may not be worth the effort.

When the time comes to do the placement, make sure you know the route and arrive on time and in the appropriate dress. Try to smile and look positive. At the end, make sure to send a letter of thanks. Leave a good impression.

'I had a brilliant time doing a week with the police and a week as a gardener in museum gardens. Both experiences were completely different but both involved meeting lots of new people, all of whom were really interesting. I'm very interested in joining the police now.'
NICHOLAS, 15

 www.thetridenttrust.org.uk for how to find a good placement.

Dear Teenager,
77 HOW TO PLAN A CAREER

I had no idea when I left school or when I left university of what I wanted to do. I'm happy I found a career in television because it has allowed me to be very nosey about other people's lives and it's good if you only have a short concentration span. I never had any grand career plan and I don't think I had ever considered working in television before I did it, and I fell into it more by accident than design. So my career advice is probably a little unconventional.

Some people know from when they are knee high to a grasshopper what they want to be (like my brother, who always knew he would be a journalist) and I have always been a little envious of their clearsightedness. If you have a goal, I think you can always reach it.

There are other people who have a very chequered career and move in and out of industries with the ease of opening and shutting a series of doors. I think that's fantastic even though it feels like the opposite of the single, goal-oriented career path. They have such variety, such novel situations and such transferable skills.

The right or wrong path depends very much on your character, your interests and your need for security and attitude to risk taking. When I think about what I want for my children, I'd like them to have a measure of financial security; a job about which they care greatly and in which they can help other people; and skills that are flexible and allow them to move either physically from one place to another or from one job situation to another. They (and you) may well have a different set of priorities. If your prime objective is to get rich quick you may view your career options differently from someone who thinks they might want to teach because they love children and they want to be able to work anywhere in the world.

It's great to know what you want and to go for it. But what you want may change at different stages in your life. Or things you had never thought of may open up for you. So when you are being asked to choose a career (which seems to happen earlier and earlier these days), don't think it's a once and forever decision. You are building up experiences, not putting yourself into a career strait-jacket.

Here are some things to think about.
● Have you considered trying to build up some work experience, offering your services as an extra pair of hands in a business in

which you are interested? You will be paid nothing but may gain the experience that buys you the job.

● If you are a graduate consider the milk round (blue-chip companies offer training, usually lasting two years, to graduates who succeed at interviews in the third year of university). Only 20 per cent of graduates get a job this way. It can be a great introduction to business, but it's not the only way.

● Follow your nose and if something interests you, do it. You may be choosing a less structured option without the same career trajectory of a blue-chip company but you may bump into completely unforeseen opportunities.

● You'll be spending a lot of your life working. If you get pleasure from it you'll have a much nicer life. Try and think out of the box. We all tend to know the careers of the people around us but maybe you should be investigating cake-making or plumbing or aircraft engineering or being a demolitions expert or being a spy or importing art or building wells in India. Don't be led by what other people think is appropriate. Do what excites you.

'I'm quite unusual in that since I was at primary school, I knew exactly what I wanted to do. I want to be a car stylist, which is someone who designs cars. I've never swayed. Plan B is to be an automotive journalist.' IAN, 19

'I think I want to be an art teacher. I worked as a teacher's assistant in the summer. I'm doing a degree in textiles and I'll see how I feel at the end of it.' MICHELLE, 19

'I don't have a career plan, I have several. I want to be an art curator, a designer and a publisher. Goodness knows what I'll actually be.' MATILDA, 20

'I have no plan. One of the joys of an arts degree is that you don't have to know exactly what you want to do yet. My dad says at his company, when he meets a graduate he wants to know if they have got a good degree from a good university and the actual subject is not the issue.' HANNAH, 20

'I've spoken to loads of people who've come out of university. They all have big debts. They went on gap years and travelled but they don't know what to do next. Now that I have spent my gap year working doing different jobs, I think I have a good idea of what employers are looking for. I've got a sense of what I want to do and how to do well.'
TOM, 19

My best advice is infinite delay on the impossible question of what do I want to do and how can I contribute to the world? People are so profligate in the way they make the decision. They make it from such a provisional and weak basis. The foundations are so pathetic. Keep your options open as long as possible. Be an observer of the world, reflect on how it works. ANTONY GORMLEY, ARTIST

Dear Teenager,
78 HOW TO COMPLETE THE PERFECT UCAS FORM

Thousands upon thousands of sixth formers apply each year for university. The decision about where to apply and the anxiety about whether you will be accepted make this feel like a momentous moment. Your hopes for the future are in the balance. Your application, called your UCAS form (Universities and Colleges Admissions Service), is submitted online in the autumn term of the year before you want to go to university Your qualifications will play a part; so too will your reference. But a crucial element of the form is one section: the personal statement. This is your sales pitch to the institutions you want to take you on.

Here is some advice on how to submit a winning form, or at the very least make yours stand out from the crowd.

● Make sure you have researched the course thoroughly.

● Go to an open day at your preferred colleges if you possibly can.

● Don't rush the form, but check the deadlines for submission and send it off in good time: earlier rather than later.

● The form needs to be in good English. Spelling mistakes and poor grammar will not help you. Make sure you prepare several drafts. Ask someone to proof-read your last draft.

● You need to put yourself in the position of the person making the selection. They have your form amidst a pile of others. What will they make of you from what you have written? Will you stand out?

The personal statement has two functions. The first is to show what an interesting, desirable human being you are and what an asset you would be to any institution. The second is to show your commitment and enthusiasm for the course for which you are applying. You only have a few paragraphs in which to demonstrate both.

On the personal front, some people are tempted to show off how fantastically multi-talented they are. They can swim up the Zambezi and play grade 8 clarinet. You undoubtedly want to demonstrate your extra-curricular talents but it's not necessarily an asset to put down that you play netball when the last time you played you were 11. Real enthusiasm shines through. State the one or two things you absolutely love to do which perhaps give a clue to your enthusiasm for the subject you have picked. Remember too that if you are applying to a college that does interviews, your personal statement will form the basis of what you are likely to talk about.

People tend to forget about the importance of the second function, that is, expressing your enthusiasm for this particular course. You need to make the staff want to teach you. If you want to study marine biology because you first went snorkelling when you were 12, then say so. If your passion to study 20th-century history grew out of your fascination for your grandfather's suitcase of war memorabilia, make this a feature.

You can buy help in writing your statement from any of dozens of websites but you shouldn't need this. Schools put a lot of effort into helping students complete these forms. That is as it should be, because they are very important. On the other hand, colleges can see when they have a set of mass-produced personal statements and it doesn't help the candidates. You need to use the form to shine out as an individual. The form needs to be polished, not cloned.

'It really, really, really doesn't matter how good your grades are. It's so much more important to be able to say that you've done stuff that's interesting. I was heavily into debating and sport and the universities want to see people who have done something, not just stayed at home and got straight A's. So many people get A's now.' TOM, 19

 www.ucas.ac.uk is the organisation through which all applications to higher education are processed.

Dear Teenager,
79 HOW TO WRITE A GOOD CV

Selling yourself is a very hard thing do to. It makes you come over all self-conscious and half of what you write seems to be bordering on an untruth. I don't mean that you should be, or are, lying, just that when you write that you are a talented musician you can start to doubt your talent. But you are selling yourself, so you do need to stand outside yourself and imagine you are reviewing someone else's good qualities.

You also need to try to make yourself stand apart. Unless you are a self-made millionaire businessman/woman aged 15, a lot of CVs look boringly similar. You need to try to find something a bit eye-catching for the recipient of your CV to catch on to. I remember my mum saying the best CV she received stated in the hobby section that the person's favourite pastime was talking to her granny. My mum immediately wanted to know why. So if you are filling in a section on hobbies and you read a lot, don't say you read a lot, say something about the authors that you like best. If you like motor-racing, say that you visit Brand's Hatch every month.

● If you are applying for a job, think about what the employer will be looking for. Read the job specification, if there is one, with great care, and give them the information they need to select you. Help them. If you want a job at a fast-food restaurant, examples of your reliability and trustworthiness would be handy. If you are applying for a job in journalism, you need to demonstrate how and when you have taken the initiative and written stories or articles.

● Make sure your school history and exam results are accurate. Recent reports suggest that a lot of people do lie and employers are being encouraged to check up more. Do not worry too much about whether you were form captain in Year 2. Think about the bigger picture and the impression you are making.

● If you think you have no relevant experience, think again. You can't claim to be a rocket scientist but a school science project might be worth offering. Regular babysitting may help suggest reliability and any other jobs you have done, however short term, will suggest initiative.

● Type your CV. Make sure the layout is clear. There are many ways of doing it. I think it is quite effective to begin with a short personal statement (only one paragraph), which summarises who you are and why you want to do whatever it is. Then you can lay out your school history. It is best to start with the most recent past and work backwards. Then you need to state relevant skills, awards and activities that will make them unable to turn you down. Proof-read it and ask someone else to read it for you.

● When you have finished preparing your CV, take a look at it as though you were the person receiving it. What would you think? Would you toss it in the bin, or would you think this person stood out?

● Tailor-make your CV for each recipient. One size does not fit all. And with the joy of the computer, that isn't a problem. Doing a CV is a bit of a drag, but imagine how much harder it used to be before computers.

● Always keep a copy of your CV and update it regularly. If you need it in a hurry you will have all the at hand.

'It's daunting. You do need help. You have to make yourself stand out from thousands of others and make yourself mega-appealing. It's really hard to be complimentary about yourself. My aunt Caroline sorted me out. She kept making me talk myself up. I felt embarrassed to say I was hard-working and diligent. I worried about sounding arrogant, but she taught me to sell myself. After all, no one else is going to!' SOPHIE, 22

COMING OF AGE

ONE OF THE EXCITING THINGS ABOUT TURNING 18 is the realisation that you are, mostly, treated as an adult and have adult privileges. You may continue to blame your mother for not breastfeeding you up to the age of 2; or you may blame your father for failing to send you to the right primary school, but life is now down to you. It is for you to shape and to make the most of whatever hand you were dealt for your childhood years.

You have the right to see 18 movies, to buy alcohol and, most importantly, to vote. As a citizen, you also have responsibilities. You have to decide what sort of person you want to be and what sort of responsibilities you want to shoulder for the community around you.

You're brilliantly lucky because if you really want to, you can go anywhere and do anything. The world is your oyster.

MINI QUIZ

Have your parents given birth to a future prime minister or a disinterested yob?

1. What sort of expression must you have for a passport photo?
2. Do you need a polling card to vote?
3. Can you be registered to vote in more than one place?

Answers

1. A neutral one.
2. No.
3. Yes, you can, if you have two residences, but you can only vote once in a general election.

Dear Teenager,
80 HOW TO GET A PASSPORT

The passport is currently regarded as the gold standard to prove you are who you say you are. Seventy-five per cent of fraudulent passport applications come from people applying for their first adult passport. These are often postal applications, sometimes from abroad. So to get yourself a first adult passport in future you will need to complete an application form and attend an interview in person with the Passport Service. You will need your birth certificate and passport photos.

Fill in the form (from the Post Office) with real care, in black ink. I stood in a queue with other applicants recently at the Passport Office and the three people nearest me all had their forms or photos returned as unsatisfactory. One girl's photo had a fringe of hair just touching an eye. Another's face was too close to the camera. The third had correctly asked a counter-signatory to sign her application but she had filled in the person's name and address herself. This is against the rules. The process is full of potential pitfalls!

The perfect passport photo
- They have to be the right size (45 mm x 35 mm) and your face has to cover 65–75 per cent of the area.
- They have to be identical.
- They have to have the right, plain background (white, light grey or cream is specified).
- If the picture is digitally produced, it needs to be 1200 dpi or better. It needs to be in focus!
- Your face has to be straight on, not in profile.
- You must not be wearing headgear nor have your face covered.
- I used to think that you weren't allowed to smile for a passport photo and that is very nearly true. You are now required to have a neutral expression with your mouth closed. So shut that mouth.
- You are also required to take off sunglasses and make sure if you wear other glasses that the frames do not cover your eyes.
- And if you wear your hair fashionably across one eye, you'll have to have a new style for the passport; no hair across eyes.

Your photo will be scanned into the back of your passport as a 'facial biometric'. If someone tries to use your passport, or puts a fake photo in a passport, the biometric won't match. As time goes on, finger-prints and iris patterns will also be added, all in order to make the passport more secure. The plan is for identity cards to be rolled out alongside passports.

When you've achieved the perfect set of pictures, you need to have them validated by a counter-signatory. If you are under 16, the validation needs to be done by someone who has known the parent or guardian who is applying for your passport for at least two years. If you are over 16, it will be someone who has known *you* for two years. This person also has to be unrelated to you and from one of the professions listed (which includes teachers, doctors, solicitors, chiropodists, journalists and funeral directors) or be someone of 'similar standing in the community'.

Leave plenty of time for your application. People all tend to apply for their passports at the same times of year (before the summer holidays) and with the huge crush of applications the whole process can grind to a halt and you can be left tearing your hair out wondering if your passport will reach you before your travel date.

When you've got your passport, try your best to keep a hold of it. Make sure you keep a note of your passport number. If you do lose it (or have it stolen) when you're abroad, contact the police and your nearest British consulate. If it goes missing at home, contact the United Kingdom Passport Office, and apply for a replacement at the same time. Losing official documents is a nightmare. Once you've got it, treasure it!

'I sent off for a passport and had my application returned. Apparently the photo was "too bright". I'd had it taken in a photo booth at a railway station but the light level was wrong. So I had to do it all over again.'
HEBE, 15

www.ukpa.gov.uk is the UK passport office site. It explains how long the process takes and how to make an urgent application.

Dear Teenager,
81 HOW TO KNOW YOUR RIGHTS

Most of us, not being lawyers, regard the law as something we try not to have much contact with. We just try to stay on the right side of it. However, there are several laws that impact on our lives and that are also there to protect our interests. Three of them are also relatively recent, and worth knowing about.

Human Rights Act 1998
The Human Rights Act brings the UK into line with the European Convention on Human Rights. Cases that relate to the Convention are now heard in UK courts instead of in Strasbourg. The Act incorporates 16 basic human rights into UK law. They include:

- right to life
- prohibition of torture
- prohibition of slavery and forced labour
- right to liberty and security
- right to a fair trial
- no punishment without law
- right to respect for private and family life
- freedom of thought, conscience and religion
- freedom of expression
- freedom of assembly and association
- right to marry
- prohibition of discrimination
- protection of property
- right to education
- right to free elections
- abolition of the death penalty.

The Act touches on diverse aspects of life. No court, local authority, tribunal or government department can make any decision that affects you without paying proper attention to your rights under the Act.

Past cases have involved decisions on which of a pair of conjoined twins should live; whether a patient in a persistent vegetative state should be fed; whether private wedding photos could be published in a celebrity magazine; whether children could be kept in secure accommodation; whether child murderers could be named; and whether a Roma family could be evicted. In my television work I frequently encounter the Act regarding people's privacy and what can or cannot be filmed. The Act lays down basic principles and is so wide-ranging that you never know when you may encounter it.

Data Protection Act 1998 and Freedom of Information Act 2005

The point of the Data Protection Act is to make sure that we all have access to information held about us by public and private organisations. The Act regulates what sort of information can be held and the circumstances in which it must be disclosed. You have the right to request to see what information is held on you whatever your age. There is an Information Commissioner's Office whose duty it is to oversee the Act. Its mission statement says it aims to 'promote public access to official information and to protect your personal information'.

You might want to know what is written in your doctor's notes; or see internal reports written about you at school or performance records kept by your employer; or check what the council has on its system about your housing needs. With certain exceptions, the Act gives you the right to demand access to these records whether on the computer or in writing. The organisation may charge a fee for providing the information. It will usually cost more for hand-written records than for those held electronically. If you decide you want some information, write to the organisation involved and ask for a Subject Access Request.

The Data Protection Act gives you access to information about yourself. If you are looking instead for information about a public authority, you need to look to the **Freedom of Information Act**.

Under this Act, public authorities are required by law to make information available under 'Approved publication schemes'. This

If you are not happy with the response to requests for information under either the Data Protection or Freedom of Information Acts, go to the Information Commissioner's website for forms for making complaints.

means they will routinely publish certain types or classes of information. However, if the information you want is not within this, you have the right to access further information (so long as it is not commercially sensitive or one of 23 other exemptions). The information should be made available within 20 days and the public authority may charge a fee. Make your request in writing.

www.clsdirect.org.uk – the Community Legal Service is there to direct you to the right source for legal information that you may need.

Dear Teenager,
82 HOW TO VOLUNTEER

Why be a volunteer? Time is precious and volunteering to do something for nothing can seem like a very low priority. Most of the reasons to do it, such as giving something back and helping your community, can sound a little worthy.

Some people fall into volunteering because of an event that happens to a friend or family. If someone you have known and loved dies of cancer, you are more likely to rattle a tin for the charity or buy the T-shirt or wear the wristband. Or, if someone you know works for a charitable organisation carrying out surgery on children with facial deformities in developing countries or performing cataract operations which restore people's sight, you're quite likely to bake cakes for their fundraiser or at least buy a strip or two of raffle tickets.

Volunteering on a more consistent basis requires a bit of effort and commitment. Although you may think about the decision whether to do it or not in altruistic terms, actually, one of the main reasons for doing voluntary work is the gain it brings you. It will broaden your horizons, increase your confidence, make you new friends, help you engage with your local community in new ways and give you great pleasure. It may well teach you new skills and help you find a job. Volunteering can take a million different forms, from visiting elderly people to conserving historic buildings.

● If you are thinking about taking a gap year, take a look at CSV (Community Service Volunteers).This is the UK's largest volunteering and training organisation and as well as part-time volunteering, they offer full-time opportunities to people aged 16 and over who can commit to between 4 and 12 months to community projects. They offer free accommodation, food and travel plus a weekly living allowance. You could work with young offenders, drug users or children with special needs. You would be living away from home, working with new people and gaining new skills. Lots of people tend to think of gap years as being in exotic locations. There is plenty of volunteer work to do here at home.

● Volunteer part time. Millennium Volunteers works nationwide and provides opportunities for volunteers between the ages of 16 and 24. You could apply to work in a school, a youth club, on a summer sports scheme. You could work with homeless people, in an old people's home or on a recycling project. You could teach dance, do art with people with learning difficulties or even dog walk and pet sit. The variety is mind-boggling. When you have decided the sort of thing you would like to do, the recruitment person contacts the charities who are looking for volunteers and you will be sent for interview ... just like a job interview. There are fewer placements available for the under-18s. You are expected to give a significant time commitment. They like you to aim for between 100 and 200 hours a year. This is not for the faint-hearted.

● The websites at the end of this section have a plethora of information about volunteering, including volunteering abroad. You can arrange to ski for a fortnight with spinally injured people or teach ICT in Africa or do work experience on a farm in Asia. Some of their information applies to volunteering part time; some of it requires you to commit to several months or a gap year. (See **How to Have a Good Gap Year**.) Again, age restrictions are likely to apply.

● Another way to be a volunteer is to sign up for the Duke of Edinburgh Award scheme. There are 225,000 people doing the awards each year. You need to be 14. There are three awards: bronze, silver and gold. It takes 6 months to get bronze, at least 12 to get silver and at least 18 for gold. You have to be a bit of an all-rounder. You have to acquire a new skill, undertake physical recreation, go on an expedition and do voluntary work. The scheme is usually run at schools or youth clubs.

● If the military appeals to you, and you're over 17, you could also join the Territorial Army. From 12 or 13 you can sign up with the Cadets.

● If all that is too full-on for you, then there are other, smaller ways of volunteering. You can take part in a fun run. You can volunteer through your school or college to help young children with their reading. You can help the old lady in the block of flats down the road with her shopping and you can make sure to buy only charity Christmas cards.

The truth of the matter is that the people who take on most have the most fun. They may be the busiest but they get the most out of life. It's not easy to think about volunteering if you could be earning instead. With student debt becoming a bigger and bigger issue, there is going to be increasing pressure on people to earn when they can. That's not good for the voluntary sector. However, looking at it selfishly, the sector may offer you experiences that you would not be able to have if you needed to be paid and those experiences might be priceless.

'What, work and not get paid for it? That doesn't make sense.'
NICHOLAS, 15

www.millenniumvolunteers.gov.uk for 16–24 year olds who want to be volunteers on a regular basis.
www.do-it.org.uk for more volunteering ideas.

Dear Teenager,
83 HOW TO VOTE

I find that going into the polling station (usually a church hall or similar building in the locality) is still a really thrilling event. It's the moment when I feel physically in touch with the democratic process, when I can impact on life around me with the stroke of a pencil.

Some people don't vote because they can't be bothered and some don't vote as a form of protest against party politics. My feeling is that the vote was hardwon and that it is one of the few acts expected of you as a citizen and you should play your part. The only British citizens who are not allowed to vote are people serving a sentence in prison and under-18s. Some people believe that voting should be mandatory. For now, it is your democratic choice.

The consensus is that young people are apathetic about politics. This might be because you are not allowed to vote until you are 18 and up until then may feel removed from the process and rather powerless. For this reason some people believe that the minimum age for voting should be 16. (The vote was given to 18 year olds in 1969.)

- Even if you choose not to vote, you are obliged by law to be on the electoral register. Each autumn, every council compiles its electoral register. A form is sent to every household for completion and a new register is published at the start of December. If you have any concerns about whether you are registered, you should contact your local town hall.

- If you are a student, you can choose where you want to be registered. A form will be sent to your home address and to your term-time address. Both need to be returned even if you do not register in both places. In a parliamentary election, you only have one vote and you can decide where you think your vote would be most useful. For local elections, you can vote in both places, whenever an election occurs. I think this is rather brilliant: you can vote tactically in the general election and get as much involved as you like in both places for local elections.

- In the future, voting may happen by telephone, by texting or by internet, to try to encourage more people to participate in polls. Right now you're a little more limited. You can vote in one of three ways: by ballot box, by post or by proxy. Voting by proxy is for special circumstances only (such as being in hospital or on remand in prison) and then you are able to instruct someone to vote on your behalf. Postal voting is much debated because it is so hard to administer and regulate. If you know you are going to be abroad, you can register to vote this way (but you no longer need a reason to vote by post, it is a question of choice).

- You will be sent a polling card before any election. Some people lose their card and then think they have no right to vote. This is not the case. You do not need this card when you go to vote. An electoral officer will tick off your name and address and give you a ballot form. You take this to a booth where, in private, you mark your vote with a cross (or 1, 2, 3 in local elections in Northern Ireland). Do not put any other marks on the ballot paper or it will not be counted.

- You don't have to be very interested in politics to vote, you just have to care enough about how your community and your country are run. But if you're passionate about politics, you have to wait until you're 21 to stand as a candidate to be a Member of Parliament. Some people think the age should be lowered to 18. After all, if you can vote for an MP at 18, perhaps you should be able to be one. The salary is pretty generous, plus allowances, but the hours are terrible. The youngest MP in the house is 26 years old.

'I voted for the first time. I'm a bit ignorant about politics, it was just a cross on a piece of paper but everyone gets a vote so I did it.'
MICHELLE, 19

'I was pleased to vote because I'd never done it before but there was nothing to it. It was rather mundane, maybe because we're in a safe constituency here and my vote wasn't going to make any difference.'
IAN, 19

'I voted at home and really I should have voted at university because the BNP are getting a hold round there and my vote would have done more good.' MATILDA, 20

 www.aboutmyvote.co.uk (the Electoral Commission's site) explains how to register.

Dear Teenager,
84 HOW TO HAVE A GOOD GAP YEAR

Some people swear by gap years. Others can't wait to go to university or start their careers. Some can't afford it or need to earn money to finance their future plans. About 50,000 people go on pre-university gap years and another 150,000 go during or after university.

For some people a year of earning money is the draw and they may continue to live at home and stash away their wages. Others use the time to try out working in an area that they think might be of future interest. Or they might want to undertake voluntary work in the community. However, most of those who go abroad say they do it for fun.

There is no right or wrong way to spend the time but it is a space in which to do a bit of growing up, and a bit of time away from exams and the rather driven atmosphere of school. As life goes on and your commitments grow, it can get harder to take time out. I didn't take my gap year until after I'd been to university and for me it was a chance to live abroad and a chance to work out what I wanted to do.

Lots of people choose to go abroad, sometimes with the intention of doing aid work in the developing world. There are companies now that specialise in finding placements for people and charge you for the privilege. People choosing this option will often work for four months to help raise the necessary funds, then take off for another two or three to an exotic location to work in a school or charitable project. However, you need to take the greatest care in finding a bona fide organisation. It is very hard to identify which they are on the internet, because they all seem to promise lots. Make

---

MIND THE GAP!

- 60% of gap year travellers are female.
- The average gap spend is £3,000.
- The average spend on kit is £150.

sure you are very clear about what you are buying. Talk to people from the organisation. Get the deal in writing. Cross-question them about accommodation, travel and work. Make sure to talk to other people who have been on a trip with the company before. Do not take anything for granted.

People worry that they won't be able to raise sufficient funds to do gap year travel, particularly now with university fees to find. But where there's a will there's a way and you should not be put off. Maybe you will have to stop buying CDs or pizzas and maybe you will have to get your hands dirty or stack shelves or serve burgers, but it's worth it for the brilliant possibilities that follow. According to *www.gapyear.com*, more unusual ways of raising funds they have heard of recently include sitting in a tree for a week; walking round Manchester dressed as a human fruit machine; and sitting in a bath of beans or a bath of cat food for a week. Flipping burgers begins to sound quite attractive! You can also find contacts for trusts that make money available to would-be gappers who have projects that fit their remit.

www.gapyear.com offers a ton of advice on what to do, where to go and how to get organised. You can also read reports from people who have just come back from gap years. It may be your first and only gap year, so you may as well draw on the experiences of others who have done it before you.

If you are planning to travel abroad on a gap year, there are a few basic do's and don'ts.

- Check out if there are any current difficulties in the country you are visiting on the Foreign Office website. Check if you need visas.
- Leave a copy of your passport and travel documents at home in case you lose them.
- Take out good insurance. Twenty-five per cent of gappers have inadequate insurance cover.
- Make sure you have the correct immunisations. (See **How to Have the Right Immunisations**).
- Always email home. Let people know you are safe so their imagination doesn't run wild.
- Don't do drugs in places where being caught with them could get you into serious bother. You don't want to land up in a foreign jail.
- If you have sex, use a condom.

- Take sensible health precautions. Wash your hands after going to the loo and before handling food. Only drink sterilised water. Avoid ice. Avoid uncooked food or food exposed to flies.
- Take your own first-aid kit with you.
- Carry toilet paper with you.
- Take half the clothes you think you need (you can always buy more locally) and make sure they are appropriate to the place you are going.

'I had a gap year. When I went to uni I was in a flat with other people who had also taken gap years and it was a lot calmer than flats where people had come straight from school. We seemed to know more what we wanted. The people without a gap year partied the hardest and did the least work. If you've had a year without sitting exams, when you go to uni you want to get on with the course.' SOPHIE, 22

'I went on a volunteer scheme for a year including teaching English in a kibbutz. It was absolutely brilliant. I can't recommend it enough. You can really tell the difference between those who have been on gap years and those who haven't.' HANNAH, 20

'Whatever you do in your gap year, even if you stay at home and do nothing, you gain a lot! Whether you are 69 or 70 doesn't make much difference but when you are 18–19 or 19–20, a year makes a big difference and you learn so much! Even if you just read, you're gaining vital experience. It's good to have a break from education too.' TOM, 19

'There's no exam at the end which is a good thing. It's great not having any system or organisation, not having to do anything. Just freedom. I went to South America for fun. Not to save the world.' GEORGE, 20

www.fco.gov.uk/knowbeforeyougo is the website of the Foreign and Commonwealth Office.
www.gapyear.com offers good advice on all aspects of taking a gap year.

Dear Teenager,
85 HOW TO GO GREEN

People of all ages should be aware of the dangers of harming our environment but when you become an adult, you take on your own set of responsibilities. You need to make sure you are doing your bit. It's too easy to blame all our troubles on the government or on foreign governments. It's up to each of us to help to create a culture and an expectation that going green makes sense. None of us wants more landfill sites or more climate change.

So what can you do? Obviously you should recycle (see **How to Recycle**). But there are a zillion other things that will help to reduce your personal burden on the environment. You can do them when you live at home and you can ensure you do them when you set up on your own.

- Turn out the lights. Don't leave the house with all your lights on.
- Don't leave TVs and computers on stand-by all day. Switch them off.
- Have a shower, not a bath and save about 40 litres of water.
- Don't over-fill your kettle. Just boil the water you need.
- Give away your old clothes that are in good condition to charity shops. Take the rest to a clothes bank.
- Take a bag with you when you go shopping instead of returning with loads of plastic bags. Some continental European supermarkets won't give you plastic bags these days. Old habits can be changed.
- Buy more fruit and veg loose from a market rather than pre-packed at the supermarket.
- Always use recycled toilet paper.
- Put up a 'No Junk Mail' sign on your door.
- Write on both sides of the paper.
- Use rechargeable batteries.
- Use long-life light bulbs (see **How to Change a Light Bulb**).
- Buy eco-friendly washing powders and washing up liquids. Use old-fashioned polish in a tin rather than an aerosol.
- Walk or cycle instead of taking a car, bus or train.

 www.foe.co.uk (Friends of the Earth) have a long, detailed list of green suggestions and contacts for help with recycling.

Dear Teenager,
86 HOW TO RECYCLE

Recycling should be second nature to us all but somehow it still isn't. In the UK, pathetically, we recycle only 11 per cent of our waste (whereas the Swedes and Germans manage to recycle 50 per cent of theirs). We carry on dumping most of our rubbish in giant landfills, which leave nasty toxins to seep into the earth; or we incinerate it and in doing so use up valuable energy and release still more toxins into the atmosphere. Clearly we need to change the way we do things to reduce our waste (see **How to Go Green**) and then we've got to be responsible about the waste we do produce. Most local authorities have their own schemes for recycling, which differ from area to area. In my area we separate glass, paper and tins from the non-recyclable rubbish. Since the scheme was introduced, it has massively reduced our black-bag waste and it's been very pleasing to see the orange bags grow. But that's not enough. Here are some other ways you could think about recycling.

● Don't junk your old mobile phones or your old glasses or your old shoes. Charities such as Oxfam arrange recycling or reuse the parts.
● Send your foreign coins and your inkjet cartridges to a charity such as the Red Cross.
● Wherever you live and work, make sure there is a scheme for paper recycling. No home, school, college or office should be without one.
● Christmas time is about the worst for waste. Not only do we generate much more party waste (30 per cent more bottles and cans) and massively more food than is sensible, but the amount of waste paper we produce rises exponentially. Think of all that wrapping paper. Open those presents carefully and reuse the paper next year. Take all your Christmas cards to a high street collection scheme. I know I should also recommend sending e-cards instead of paper Christmas cards – but call me old fashioned – I'm not very fond of them. Instead, I would recommend only sending cards to people far away whom you're not going to see.
● Use *www.freecycle.org* to donate unwanted items to someone in your area or to find things you could use. Your rubbish is their treasure and vice versa.

Recycling really is a case where you and I as individuals can make a real impact on the global environment. So do it.

 www.freecycle.org tells you how to offer and get hold of all kinds of stuff for free.
www.redcross.org and **www.oxfam.org.uk** for donations to shops and collections of coins, mobile phones, etc.
www.recycle-more.co.uk for information about recycling.

Dear Teenager,
87 HOW TO BE CHARITABLE

You may be hard pushed to pay your own bills, but there's always someone worse off than you. Most people don't like the idea of accepting charity but those in desperate situations rely on other people's generosity because they have no other option. One of the problems of the modern world is charity fatigue. We see so much suffering on the TV that we glaze over and aren't moved to give any more. We see a mass of familiar suffering and fail to see the individual who needs help.

To whom should you be charitable? Obviously the cause is down to you. I don't think it's a good idea to give to beggars because it encourages begging and, beyond the next drink or meal, doesn't improve the lot of the beggar. I don't think you should give to people who come asking at the door. I feel slightly threatened by strangers coming to my front door and you have no way of knowing that they actually represent the organisation they say they do. I don't think you should give to unauthorised sellers of the *Big Issue*. It queers the pitch for bona fide *Big Issue* vendors who deserve support because the foundation really helps homeless people.

Gift Aid

When you become a tax payer, there is a way of maximising your gift to a charity. It is called Gift Aid and you have probably seen the Gift Aid declarations in places where you are asked to make donations. As a non-tax payer, or without the declaration, your gift of a pound is worth a pound to the charity. If you pay tax and fill in the form, your pound is worth £1.28. When you become mega-successful and become a higher-rate tax payer, you can even claim back a further 23p for every pound (which you can choose to donate or to claim back in your tax return).

Gifts that really help

We're all guilty, especially at Christmas, of buying more tat than we all need and wrapping up fancy parcels and giving them to each other. Meanwhile other people are starving and homeless. In recent years a new form of gift giving has emerged. Instead of buying a conventional present, you can make a donation to a charity on the other person's behalf. These donations can take interesting forms. Goats have proved very popular. I like the idea of buying a Kalashnikov rifle, which will be turned into hoes or axe heads for farmers in war-ravaged Sierra Leone. The person to whom you're sending the gift receives a card telling them about the donation. You can try and make a match with the recipient, for example sending a gift of 100 school dinners in Africa to a teacher, or buying a first-aid kit for an orphanage for a friend training to be a nurse. It's got to be better than a box of bath salts, hasn't it?

'At my school all the teachers decided not to send each other Christmas cards and to give the money instead to a school in Sri Lanka that was struck by the tsunami. It was a much better idea.' NICHOLAS, 15

www.goodgifts.org is a good place to choose a gift that can make a real difference. This website offers a wide range of charitable gifts that you can buy on behalf of family and friends. The gifts include goats for communities in recovering war zones and groves of spring-flowering trees for UK cities www.oxfamunwrapped.com offers fun, unusual and life-changing gifts that range from mosquito nets to camels to tanks that hold enough safe water for 1,000 people. Prices range from £5 to £20,000.

LIVING AWAY FROM HOME

MOVING AWAY CAN BE TRAUMATIC OR GREAT FUN, or both. Some people have it much easier than others. If you are moving to a university hall of residence, you are lucky. You won't have to deal with difficult landlords, your repairs will be done and you may well have a canteen with your meals laid on. If you are moving away on your own to a room or a shared flat, things can be trickier. You've not only got to cope with looking after yourself but with living with other people in a new environment. And with no mum to pick up your washing. Hopefully it will be a great new adventure and, with a bit of training at home before you go, you'll rise to the challenge.

MINI QUIZ

Are you an independent spirit or are you tied to your parents' apron strings?

1. How many meals a month do you cook currently?
2. Have you ever done paid work?
3. Is a gap year a good thing?

Answers

1. If the answer is fewer than four, you need to get cooking.
2. If you haven't, you probably have a lot to learn about budgeting as well as managing your time.
3. There's no right or wrong answer to this, but you should consider the possibilities. A gap year can make you feel more independent.

Dear Teenager,
88 HOW TO ASSEMBLE FLAT-PACK FURNITURE

I am congenitally incapable of assembling a flat-pack. Just as I could never read an exam question all the way through before starting, I can't read the instructions on a flat-pack. I panic. My friend Delia is the queen of the flat-pack and likes nothing better than the challenge of one she hasn't done before. She eyes up the carton, her pupils enlarge at the sight of the Swedish instructions, and she's off.

When I was growing up, if you bought an item of furniture, a large van would drive up to the door and a pair of men in overalls would get out and carry your purchase into the house. If they cleared away the wrapping you'd give them a tip but when they left, your bookcase or table or desk would be ready to use. That is now history. Unless you are super-rich, most of what you buy is going to be flat-pack and you will be much better off following Delia's example than mine.

Here is Delia's guide to becoming a successful flat-packer.

● Pour yourself a coffee or a Coke. This is a process to enjoy. Savour the pleasure. This is fun, not torture.

● The secret is all in the preparation. Read through ALL the instructions to the end. This is critical. People who launch into Stage 1 without reading ahead end up in a shambles. You may find when you get to Stage 4 you need to hold something and glue a dowel in at the same time and you need to recruit an extra pair of hands. You need to know this upfront.

● Make sure you have all the tools you need in front of you. The instructions will tell you exactly what is required.
● Empty all the little plastic bags into neat rows on the floor. Make sure everything is there and matches the instructions. Double check now.

● Now you can begin. And it will go like clockwork.

Believe it or not, people have actually set up businesses putting up other people's flat-packs so if you learn the tricks of the trade now you will certainly save yourself anguish later on, and, if you are enterprising, you may have created a career opportunity.

Dear Teenager,
89 HOW TO DEAL WITH A LANDLORD

If you rent a room or a flat, you will be making a legal agreement with the landlord and there are rights and responsibilities on both sides of the contract. Often, people are in such a hurry to find a nice place to live that they feel they haven't got time to read between the lines. But the devil is in the detail.

You may love somewhere you've seen and you may be anxious that you'll lose it if you don't sign on the dotted line right now. Don't do it. Wait. Check the tenancy agreement with care. There are plenty of standard ones you can find on the internet to compare. If you are a student, you may also be able to check with the Student Advice Centre. Question the landlord on anything you are dubious about. You can always ask for an amendment.

You will probably be signing a fixed term contract, which means that you are obliged to pay the rent for the duration even if you choose to leave earlier, so be clear about how long you want to stay and do not sign up to something that does not suit your needs. The names of all the tenants will probably be on the contract. If that is the case, and one tenant leaves early, you are jointly responsible, so the landlord will come after the rest of you for the shortfall.

Things you should ask a prospective landlord before signing:

● When and how is the rent payable?

● How long is the lease and is it renewable?

● When were the gas and electrics last checked? Ask to see the certificates.

● How can the landlord be contacted if there is a problem? Make sure you have their address as well as a phone number.

● Would you have any unexpected responsibilities, such as looking after a garden?

● Are there any limitations on what you can do in the house, such as smoking or putting up pictures on the walls?

● Which bills would you be responsible for and how much are they likely to be?

Things a landlord is likely to ask you:

● You will most likely be asked for a guarantor. This is the person who will be asked to pay up if you default on your rent.

● You will be asked for a deposit, which is usually equivalent to a month's rent. If you are letting through an agency, they will keep the deposit until any disputes are settled. Changes to the law are expected which may make all landlords place the deposit with a third party.

What are the landlord's responsibilities?

● The landlord has to maintain the house and sort out problems within a reasonable time frame.

● The landlord is responsible for the safety of the electrical installations and of the fire safety of the furniture and fittings.

● Any gas appliances must be checked annually by a CORGI-registered practitioner and the tenant must be given the certificate. Between 30 and 40 people in the UK die each year from carbon monoxide poisoning, so servicing of appliances is a serious issue.

● The landlord must provide working fire alarms on every floor.

● The landlord must inform you in advance if he or she wants to visit. He or she cannot invade your privacy.

What are your responsibilities?

● You must pay your rent on time. You could make life easier and pay it by standing order (so that the bank pays it automatically on an agreed day each month).

● You should read the electricity and gas meters on arrival and ensure that both you and the landlord have a copy.

● You should either ask for or make a total inventory of the furnishings and their condition. Also check and make note of the condition of the building itself. Both you and the landlord should have a signed copy. If anything is broken or damaged, make a note of it or take a photo in case there is an argument about it when you leave.

● Don't mess with fire extinguishers or block fire escapes. This is critical for your safety and helps fulfil your side of the contract.

● You must allow the landlord reasonable access. This is usually with 24 hours' notice.

● You must look after the property and promptly report any faults to the landlord.

● You must fulfil any obligations in your tenancy agreement, which is why it is a good idea to read it properly.

Landlords, like anyone else, can be nice or nasty people. If you think you may have got a dodgy landlord, make particularly sure that you make notes of the conversations you have and put the results of the conversation in writing to him or her and keep a copy. (See **How to Complain**.) If you have a complaint, try to deal with it rationally and courteously with the landlord first. If the problem isn't rectified, take further advice (from a students' union or the Citizens Advice Bureau or the local council). If you have a dispute, do not stop paying the rent or you could be evicted. Make sure that you have fulfilled your side of the contract.

The laws that govern landlords and tenants are complex. If you're getting into deep water, take advice.

'I didn't know that if all of you sign the tenancy agreement, then you're liable if someone doesn't pay their rent. So who you chose to move in with is a really serious decision. You have to be sure they'll pay their part of the bills. If one flatmate moves out or just doesn't pay, the landlord comes after the people who have been paying. Everyone's in a rush to get their flats sorted out and you feel there's pressure to sign. Be very wary about who your flatmates are. And be wary of dodgy landlords.' SOPHIE, 22

 www.nusonline.co.uk offers useful advice on landlords, contracts and halls of residence.

Dear Teenager,
90 HOW TO SHARE A FLAT

When you leave home you may be going to a hall of residence at a university. There are lots of advantages to that. You may have meals available on site. Cleaners may keep the common areas clean. You are likely to be close to friends and some people like living communally. But many more people both at university and in the world of work will find themselves in shared accommodation, and some actively prefer it. In a shared flat, you can forge friendships that last a lifetime or you can create a battleground around money and organisation.

If you want a peaceful life, here are some ground rules you should follow.

● Think about where the accommodation is. Are transport facilities reasonable? Will you feel safe or scared approaching the house or flat at night? Does the accommodation feel secure? Student flats are often easy pickings for burglars … not very secure and full of electrical goods.

● Think about the people you will be living with. This is a hard one because people are often different when you move in with them. Are they people who have a similar attitude to cleanliness and to bill paying? Can you talk to them about things they do that bother you? Will you be able to discuss how you feel if someone has a partner staying over most nights who hogs the bathroom?

223

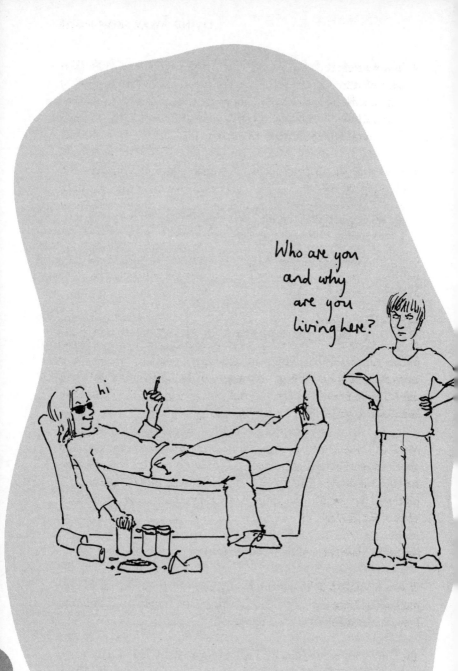

● If you are renting with a group of friends, you need to be clear who has the responsibility for the rental and what happens if someone decides to leave. If they move on in the middle of the year and the TV licence has six months to run, will you refund their share or expect them to pay it?

● How will you divide up meal preparation and shopping and cleaning? Who will deal with any issues that arise with the landlord? Can you depend on your flatmates to pay up their share of the rent on time?

Some of the friends you make now are likely to be people you'll hope never to have to share a bathroom with again. Others are likely to be friends for life.

'On an emotional level, I wish I had known that you can't be liked by everybody. Everyone at school gets on really well. But at university, it's so intense it's like being on Big Brother. You don't have your parents to moan at or to reassure you that you're still a nice person, so the tensions build up. At university, you have only just met people. At home, friends and family have known you all your life. It's a big difference.' MATILDA, 20

'It's a nightmare trying to organise a flat. There's always someone who does bugger all. In my experience girls bleat about stuff and complain behind one another's backs. If they try to do something about it, it's always in a very polite, timid sort of way, "Do you think you could possibly ...?" With blokes we get angry and shout at each other. Then there are no more problems. It's less important whether you've got an en-suite bathroom than whether you're with mates.' ED, 21

'If you buy loo rolls for a shared flat, always keep back a roll in your room. I don't know what happens to loo rolls in shared houses but the best piece of advice I have is to keep your own stash!' SOPHIE, 22

'Even though we were sharing, I bought my own food and had my own cupboard. Silly things like milk, butter and sugar we should have shared but didn't. We all bought our own. Next year I hope I get on better with new flatmates and then it would be useful to share.' MICHELLE, 19

THE RULES ABOUT TV LICENCES

● One of your responsibilities when you move away from home is the TV licence. If you have a TV or a VCR or set-top box or DVD recorder or a PC with a broadcast card (in other words any equipment to receive or record programmes), you need a licence.

● You are not covered by your parents' licence at home. If you share a house with a separate tenancy agreement, you need your own licence for the TV in your room.

● If you have a joint tenancy agreement and a single TV shared by all, then you probably only need one licence. Do not assume it is your landlord's responsibility.
If you live in a student hall of residence, each student needs their own licence for their room.

● If you are a student and pay for a licence in October and do not stay on over the summer, you may be entitled to a rebate for the unused quarter.
You can be fined £1,000 for failing to have a licence. Check if you need one by calling 0870 241 5973 (or 0870 242 1417 for students). You can buy a licence on-line at www.tvlicensing.co.uk.

'Going from being an only child to living in a flat with four people with very different attitudes to food, bills and cleaning was mad. You certainly learn social skills. You have to tolerate people's failings much more when you live with them. All hell can break loose!' STEVE, 26

 When I went to RADA, I couldn't get a grant, so I lived in squats for a year. It was awful. You never knew who you were going to wake up next to in the morning. I just went around with my sleeping bag on my back. One night I went to stay at a mate's house. I went on the bus and pretended to be asleep to avoid *paying my fare. But then I did fall asleep for real and went all the way to the end of the line. By the time I got back to my friend's house it was too late to knock and wake up the landlady. So I went over the road and slept on the steps of a block of flats. When I woke up in the morning, my sleeping bag and I were under a foot of snow.*

The next year I got a scholarship and got a room. It was luxury.

GARY MAVERS, ACTOR
(DR MANNING IN *CASUALTY* AND
DR ATTWOOD IN *PEAK PRACTICE*)

Dear Teenager,
91 HOW TO COPE WITH HOMESICKNESS

When you leave home it is an abrupt change for everyone. After all, you've probably been at home (even if home has moved) for the past 16 to 18 years, long enough to get used to it. For some people it is a relief to get out. For most, it will be a mixture of feelings: there will be hope and excitement about life ahead and a little fear of the unknown. And there will be a sense of loss of all that is familiar and dear.

But it isn't for ever. Before long you'll be back with tales to tell. Your relationship with your parents will be different. You may find you don't even take home for granted! Don't look at going away as a permanent exit, just another stop on a journey.

● It will take you a while to develop new routines and to cope with the myriad new things around you. Give yourself a bit of space. Don't rush back the first weekend, even if you have got a basket of laundry. Settle in, take your time and ring home, but not every single day.

● Remember that lots of other people around you are likely to be new too. It's a good time to try to join things in which you have an interest. You can always drop them if you don't like them but give them a go now.

- Make sure you are keeping a balance between work and play and don't get over-exhausted by constantly staying up into the small hours. We all feel more fragile when we are tired.

- Don't expect too much. A complete social life and a brilliant career (work or academic) may not blossom in the first week anyway. If you're feeling that being away is not all it promised to be, then home will start to have an even greater allure. Try to look forward, not back.

- It's always a good thing to talk to other people. You don't have to put a brave face on it. Talk to others in the same boat if you can. If you are away at university there will also be tutors and student union people you can talk to. Ask for and accept help if you can. If you are feeling depressed, see your GP and look for a professional counsellor.

A third of students going away to university admit to feeling homesick. Most of them end up having a great time. So can you.

'Leaving home was hard, not having friends and not having family to support you. The first month was the worst. Everything was so new. I found it tough. I called home a lot but the best thing I did was not to go home. I coped by speaking to them but if I had gone home at first I wouldn't have wanted to have come back!' MICHELLE, 19

'I lived in hall for my first year. I don't feel I've joined the real world yet. Living in was an intermediate step with its regular mealtimes. Life hasn't descended into chaos yet which it will now that I'm moving into a flat. It was a good thing to be in hall first. Good for meeting friends too.' GEORGE, 20

'People go on about it being the best years of your life but it's actually very stressful at the beginning. It's much harder than people make out. Don't call home too much. It's good not to rely on speaking to your parents every day. It's time for you to spread your wings. You need to reassure your parents that you're OK but calling them can make you home-sick.

I'm so glad that someone told me that Freshers' Week is horrible. If you didn't know that you might want to go home, thinking that everyone but you is having a good time.' HANNAH, 20

'I've been away from home before for two weeks max on holiday. But within the first week of being away you adapt. Everyone's dumped in it. It's a lot of help being with people in the same boat.' OLLIE, 18

I was at an approved school, a school for bad boys. One day I had a visit from my mother. She brought biscuits for me and when I ate them I felt so homesick that I decided I had to run away. This place was in the middle of the forest and I was a city boy. I ran and I was so scared. It was late afternoon and I ran. At night-time, I leant against a tree and slept standing up for a few hours. I carried on running. I got to an opening and saw a road. And there in front of me was the approved school. I had gone round in a big circle. I was so hungry and disillusioned with my attempt that I went back in. The moral? Young boys should all have a compass!

BENJAMIN ZEPHANIAH,
POET AND NOVELIST

HUNGRY FOR LIFE

MY CHILDREN THINK OF THE KITCHEN simply as the source of snacks, 24/7. That will change when they take charge of one of their own or one that they share. Rotting rubbish, unwashed dishes, mould-infested fridges and food that's well past its sell-by date are likely to fill them with nostalgic thoughts for home...

Children should of course all learn to cook. Home-made food is cheaper and more enjoyable than processed. You don't need to be a gourmet chef but you do need to acquire some basic competencies. This book isn't the place for recipes. With Jamie Oliver and TV chefs galore and student cook-books, there are plenty of sources of help. I have only included some fast food comfort eating as well as a very easy cake to round off any celebration.

Establishing a few good habits while at home will help you later. It should be second nature for children to clear the table and load the dishwasher after meals. (I say it should be, I can't swear that it's entirely second nature round here.) Responsibility should go further than that. Children and husbands shouldn't only put the bins out when they are so instructed. The dishwasher shouldn't only be unloaded by over-18s.

? MINI QUIZ

Are you a budding domestic god or goddess, or are you a couch potato?

1. What do you do before handling food?
2. What can you never put in a microwave?
3. Which day of the week do your bin men come?

Answers

3. Shame on you if you don't know.

2. Anything metal.

1. Always wash your hands but do not then spoil your model behaviour by drying them on the tea-towel.

Shopping should be a shared responsibility by the whole family. And pigs might fly.

I made a few basic rules. No one can leave the kitchen until a meal has been cleared. Anyone who takes plates or glasses away from the kitchen has to return them and clear them away or be banned from taking food or drink to those rooms ever again. Some people recommend a household rota. I've never been able to make one stick but the principle is appealing. Parents, be as draconian as you can (it's cruel to be kind). Teenagers, get off your backsides and scrub that pan!

'I was a very domesticated child. But then again I was a girl in an Asian family. I can cook very well. Most of it I learnt at home through family recipes. Meals at home used to be strictly timetabled events, which required every member to be seated together at least once a day. That changed when I came to college. Although meals have not been a problem for me because I eat in college-hall, I was very excited at being able to sit in bed, watch some movies and eat spaghetti.' ASHLEIGH, 18

'I like being able to eat dinner at 10 o'clock at night if I want to. No one's going to stop me.' IAN, 19

'You have to look out for one another. You haven't got parents around to help. In my flat it's like a little family now. On Sundays we sit down and have a roast together.' ED, 21

Dear Parents,

The earlier your children start to cook, the better. I know because I failed. Mine have always assumed that I'm the cook and their role is to eat. I am having a battle to get them into the kitchen now and regret not having made them take part earlier in food preparation. I'm suggesting to my children that they cook a family meal every weekend and I have made it a (relatively unambitious) goal that they each know how to produce a couple of dishes that will feed them and their friends cheaply and happily. Mince or a tomato sauce are ideal. They learn a basic cooking technique and the satisfaction of a meal now and more in the freezer for a later date.

'We did lots of cooking together. It was good to be able to do it, to try out things. It's good to know how to cook before you go. Once you are sharing a flat, you feel a bit embarrassed if you haven't got some vague skills.' ANNA, 24

Dear Teenager,
92 HOW TO SHOP FOR FOOD

The key thing about going shopping is to make a list. If you don't think about what you need you'll spend a fortune and still come home with nothing to eat. If you can plan ahead for meals across the next week, or at least some of them, you can buy what you need.

It's better to go and do a big supermarket shop once a week than to keep running up the road to the corner shop, which will be pricier. Supermarkets often sell off fresh food more cheaply at the end of the day. When you go to a supermarket, look out for what's on offer, including BOGOFs (buy one get one free). If you're a Weetabix person and the large packs are on special offer, it makes sense, of course, to buy the large pack now rather than wait until you need some more and the offer has finished. And if you run out of cash, you can always eat it for your evening meal.

If you're in shared accommodation, it can be advantageous to find a way of pooling your funds for shopping so that you can buy store cupboard items and take advantage of deals on bigger sizes.

Don't be over-ambitious and think you're going to cook five gastronomic meals in a row. Chances are you'll do the first meal, then find better things to do the next night and the food will grow mould in the fridge. I am often guilty of this.

If you don't keep track of what you've already got in your fridge, going shopping can become a giant guessing game. There's nothing worse than going to the fridge to retrieve that nice piece of cheddar you were looking forward to, only to find it has gone mouldy, or that you have in fact already drunk the orange juice you are convinced was in there.

If you are planning to freeze food, do so on the day you buy it. Always store the food you buy correctly. There is no point buying biscuits and leaving the packet open allowing them to go soft; store them in a tin.

FOOD TO BUY FOR YOUR STORE CUPBOARD

Don't be a Mother Hubbard. Stock these items to ensure you have always got a meal close at hand.
Olive oil
Tinned tomatoes
Tins of tuna
Pasta (different shapes)
Rice
Salt, pepper, selection of dried herbs
Pesto sauce
Tinned sweetcorn
Breakfast cereal
Bread, orange juice and cartons of soup in the freezer compartment of the fridge if you have one.

ESSENTIAL ITEMS FOR COOKING UP A TREAT IN YOUR KITCHEN

These are the things you really should have in your kitchen. For comfort and pleasure you can add to the list, but these are the basic necessities.
A kettle
A good sharp knife
A pan
A wooden spoon
A cheese grater
Some plastic, airtight containers which you can put your name on
Silver foil
All-purpose disinfectant kitchen spray
Some disposable cloths
Washing up liquid
Bin bags

Freshly grown organic food is usually the tastiest and the most expensive. Savacentre or Lidl type stores are usually the cheapest. The trick is to buy and cook wisely. Here are some clues.

● A whole uncooked chicken is cheaper to buy than a couple of chicken breasts.

● Organic chicken is very pricey but try to go for the free-range chickens because they have a lot more taste than the battery ones. And they have had a better life.

● Don't buy fresh pasta; it's a waste of money. The dry stuff is fine.

● Don't buy puddings, especially not individual ones. They are expensive, small and bad for you. Have fruit instead, or yogurt.

● When buying yogurt, buy a big pot of natural yogurt and use it over several nights. You can add brown sugar or fruits to it. Or eat it with a shortbread biscuit.

● Potatoes, rice and pasta are all versatile and cheap. So are baked beans. These are all good staples.

● Don't even think about buying ready-made meals or TV dinners. The closest you should get to this is soup, which is cheap and filling. Ready-made meals are over-priced, usually bad for you and quite often disappointing. Lots of them are made from reconstituted meat, the thought of which is enough to turn your stomach.

'I never realised how often you had to go to the supermarket. And I never realised how heavy the shopping bags are! Or how much time it all took up.' ANNA, 24

'I enjoy going shopping and stuff like that. I can see how much I've changed! When I go back home now and see my friends who still live there, I feel much more independent than them.' IAN, 19

'The two things I couldn't live without when I left home were a toaster and a kettle. I couldn't do without tea and toast.' MATILDA, 20

Dear Teenager,
93 HOW TO UNDERSTAND FOOD LABELS

Food labelling has become a very sophisticated and often misleading affair. Products are beautifully packaged and words shine out at us encouraging us to buy. It's fresh, it's pure, it's natural. It is farmhouse premium, finest, value or economy. Most of these words have no legal definition so they only give you the impression the manufacturer is striving for. Sometimes they can be misleading. Products can scream out that they are low in fat but turn out to be sky high with salt. You have to read a label carefully.

WHAT YOU MIGHT FIND ON FOOD LABELS

● **No added sugar or unsweetened:** no sugar has been added but the product may well contain natural sugars. Always look for cordials with no added sugar.

● **Low sugar:** must contain no more than 5% sugar per 100 g/100 ml.

● **Reduced sugar:** must contain 25% less sugar than the standard product.

● **Organic:** must be produced according to European laws on organic production. Not every single ingredient is organic but 95% of the listed ingredients will be.

● **Red Tractor:** this is the mark of the Farm Assurance Scheme and the product has been produced on a farm registered with the scheme.

● **Union Jack flag:** produced, processed and packed in the UK.

(continued overleaf)

● **Display until:** this is intended for the shopkeeper for stock control. For the customer, it is the Best Before date that matters.

● **Best Before:** you are unlikely to die of food poisoning if you eat something a day or so after its Best Before date. It may be past its peak of freshness but you will survive. Don't risk it, however, with eggs. Eggs may contain salmonella bacteria, which may start to multiply, and they can make you sick.

● **Light or lite:** this has no legal standing and doesn't relate to any particular measure. Something may advertise itself as 'lite', but turn out to be no lighter than a rival brand.

● **Low fat:** this indicates that the food contains less than 3 g fat per 100 g/100 ml of the food.

● **Reduced fat:** the food must contain 25% less fat than a similar standard product. But beware, it does not mean that the product is low fat.

● **Less than 5% fat or 95% fat free:** this means that if you have bought yourself a ready-made meal with a 400 g portion, the meal will contain 20 g of fat. You then need to compare that figure with the daily recommended allowance.

● **Polyunsaturates and monounsaturates:** these are fats that can help reduce blood cholesterol levels and reduce the risk of heart disease. It is better to eat these and to cut down on saturated fats.

● **Salt or sodium chloride:** salt is made from sodium chloride but the two are measured differently. To convert salt to sodium chloride, divide by 2.5; to convert from sodium to salt, multiply by 2.5. The government recommends a daily allowance of 6 g of salt a day for adults.

It's all a bit like learning a foreign language – food manufacturers' language – but it's important to have a grasp of it even if you're not totally fluent.

 www.kidshealth.org has a good section on how to read the nutrition contents of labels.
www.eatwell.gov.uk, the Food Standards Agency site, has information on every food labelling term under the sun.

Dear Teenager,
94 HOW TO FILL A FRIDGE

The fridge in our house is a magnet both for people and for argument. Everyone goes and helps themselves from its contents and expects it to be constantly replenished. This gives me grief because I can never find the one thing I want because someone has eaten it. It also gives me grief because people can't be bothered to wrap things properly after use and I'm always finding dried-up bits of food that would have been perfectly good if the foil had been wrapped tightly round them, instead of torn off and stuffed back on top afterwards. The fridge also irritates my husband because he thinks the rest of us are incapable of storing things in an orderly manner (and he's right).

Things only get more complicated if you try and share a fridge with other people. Go into any office with a fridge and you will probably pass out at the disgusting smells emanating from it. Somebody's lunch from three months ago and cartons of rancid milk will be sharing the space with today's sandwiches.

Each time we empty our fridge and start over I feel a sense of optimism and control. We have instituted some better fridge management habits and I can recommend them. If you don't want to get food poisoning, there are also some basic rules.

● Always refrigerate food that says it needs to be kept in the fridge and do so as quickly as possible. Make sure that it is well wrapped. Food that is not wrapped will shrivel; ham goes all crinkly and dark and cheese goes hard and cracked.

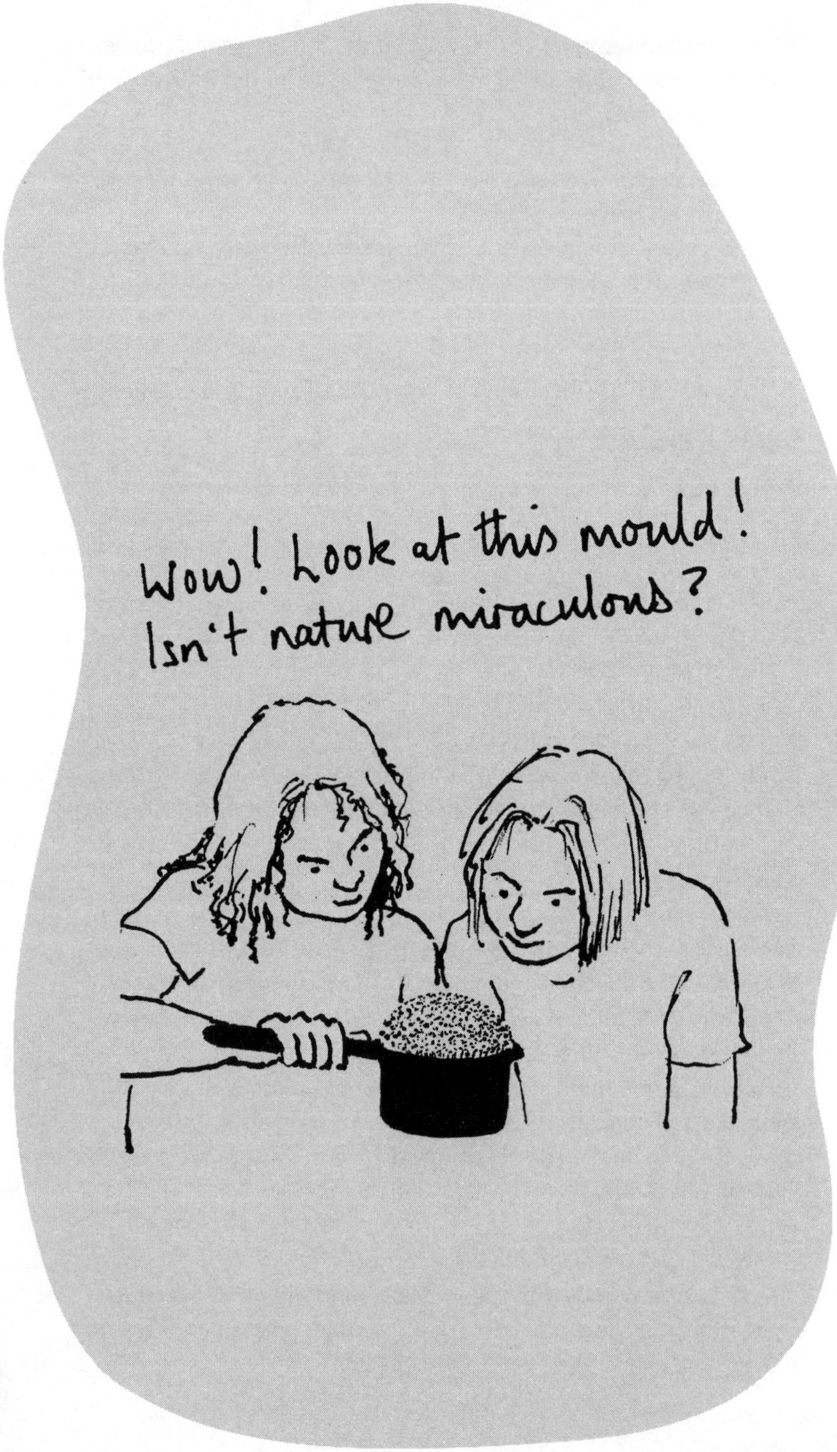
Wow! Look at this mould!
Isn't nature miraculous?

- If you are putting uncooked meat in the fridge, put it at the bottom in a sealed container so that it won't drip on to other food and contaminate it. Don't eat it long after its 'use-by' date.

- If you have cooked meat, keep it separate from raw meat or fish.

- Don't put garlic or onions in the fridge or everything will reek of them. Don't put avocados or bananas in either because they turn brown and go soggy.

- Try and establish some kind of organisation in the fridge, whether that is by person or food type. I've never been much good at this, although I do find it very satisfying to know that the cheese is always in the same place.

- Empty your fridge every few weeks to stop it becoming a disaster area. When I say empty, I mean empty it completely, not just shuffle around a few bottles and remove one dodgy bag. Wipe the shelves and pockets with a damp cloth, clear away all the crumbs and spills, then refill. There are fancy fridges you can buy, which have a first- in, first-out mechanism so that you automatically reach for the oldest milk rather than the freshest. I've never seen one but I think a bit of common sense can probably do just as well. Your nose will tell you if the milk has been there for more than a week.

'Six of us shared a fridge. One girl would buy a whole week's shopping and stuff it in the fridge. It was very difficult. Then something would smell and I'd have to clear the fridge out. Once someone left a cucumber in the bottom. It had fermented so much that juice was running round the tray. I don't even like cucumbers when they are fresh!'
MICHELLE, 19

'Shared fridges can be a nightmare as you have to look at everyone else's delicious food on their shelf, when all you are left with is some margarine and an elderly tomato on yours. One of my housemates always has a well-stocked shelf and sometimes he catches me looking at it longingly. If he catches me and is feeling generous he will sometimes cook for me, too. Result!' RACHEL, 20

Dear Teenager,
95 HOW TO FREEZE FOOD

If you know how to use the freezer you will be making life much easier for yourself. Chances are, if you live in rented accommodation or in a hall of residence, you will have access to one. If you have a freezer, you have always got breakfast. If you cook food for yourself you can eat a portion and put the rest in the freezer. It's fantastic having a home-cooked meal ready and waiting for you. It's also fantastic for stand-bys when you have nothing else to eat. Fish fingers, oven chips and peas is our staple freezer meal!

● You can put a sliced loaf in the freezer and keep it for a month. Pull it out and you can make toast. Ditto with crumpets or muffins. Keep a store of long-life OJ and you are made. Life always seems bearable if you have a good breakfast.

● When you cook – whether it's a simple pasta sauce, mince or soup – always cook some for the freezer. It makes life so much simpler to have food ready prepared. You'll find the food tastes better second time round when you haven't had to cook it!

● Freeze your food either in freezer bags or in plastic tubs such as old ice cream or yogurt containers. When you package it, think what number of portions suits you best. If you want to eat it yourself on three separate occasions, remember to freeze the food in three separate parts. (If you freeze it altogether you have to defrost it altogether.)

● Soup that you find in the chiller cabinet does well in the freezer and is a very useful stand-by. Some things are good for freezing and some things are bad. Bad things include salad vegetables, whole eggs, spaghetti, boiled potatoes, yogurt and mayonnaise.

'I've just bought quarter-price food from the supermarket to put in the freezer. One thing my mum taught me was to buy loads of bread if it's on offer and put it in the freezer. You take a loaf out in the morning, put it on the sideboard and when you come back in the evening, it's ready to eat.' KACHENGA, 19

FOUR FREEZER RULES

● Freeze things straight after you have bought them or made them. Always freeze on the same day.

● Label everything. It's astonishing how difficult it is to work out whether it's a bag of chilli con carne or mincemeat that you have extracted from the back of the freezer. It's also surprising how quickly you forget when you put something in. So date it. Most cooked dishes such as chilli con carne can be kept in the freezer for three months.

● Once thawed, do not freeze again, or indeed reheat more than once. You don't want to poison yourself or your friends.

● Raw meat should be defrosted thoroughly before cooking. When you want to eat a frozen, previously cooked dish, you can thaw it (a good way is to leave it in the fridge overnight) or cook it from frozen but the cooking time will then be much longer.

'Watch out for freezer burn. Once I caught a fish. A big one, a 14 pounder. I put it in the freezer and it stuck to the bottom. I had to cut it off with a knife. A saw would have been easier. The moral of the story is, always wrap things up before you put them in the freezer.' MICHAEL, 15

Dear Teenager,
96 HOW TO AVOID FOOD POISONING

There are more than nine million cases of gastroenteritis in the UK each year and it is on the increase. Gastroenteritis is an inflammation of the gut and is very often the result of food poisoning. It leads to vomiting and diarrhoea. Not nice. And it is most often avoidable.

Avoiding food poisoning comes down to hygiene. All those things your mother used to tell you about washing your hands were for a reason. Here are the ten basic rules to staying healthy around food.

1. Always wash your hands after going to the toilet and before touching food. Also wash them after gardening, and after touching raw meat. And wash them again if you've been stroking the dog or the cat.
2. Don't dry them on the tea towel (see **How to Wash and Dry Up**). You don't want to spread the bugs around.
3. Make sure your kitchen is clean. Have clear surfaces and spray some antibiotic spray with a clean, fresh cloth.
4. If you're cutting up raw meat, have a dedicated board on which to do it. You don't want to cut an apple up next on the same surface. Raw meat may contain bacteria and you don't want to pass it around.
5. Put your raw meat and fish, well wrapped up, in the bottom of the fridge. (See **How to Fill a Fridge**.)
6. Always keep perishable food in a cool place. Use it when it is as fresh as possible.
7. Rinse your fruit and vegetables before eating. You don't know how many chemicals and how many hands have touched them.
8. If you are defrosting food, do it thoroughly (see **How to Freeze Food**).
9. If you are re-heating food, make sure it is properly cooked all the way through. Bugs love to proliferate in tepid food.
10. Keep those pets away. Fido might be fun but his place isn't in the kitchen when you're preparing food.

If you do get ill, go to bed and rest. Make sure you keep drinking lots of water and a little fruit juice. If you feel really bad, ask someone to bring you a rehydration drink (from any chemist). This salt solution replenishes the body. When you feel like eating, have some soup or some rice or pasta. We used to have a spaniel which was often sick because of eating rubbish found in the street and he always recovered quickest eating rice. It worked for him, it will work for you! But make sure, again, that you wash your hands and stay away from other people's food. Gastroenteritis spreads alarmingly easily and your friends won't thank you for it.

www.nhsdirect.nhs.uk for guidance on what to do if you think you have food poisoning.

Dear Teenager,
97 HOW TO COOK WITH A MICROWAVE

Microwave cooking is brilliant because it is quick, easy and the food it produces is good for you. It can also be cheaper to use than a conventional oven. It involves the initial outlay for the machine itself but if you learn to do more than heat up ready meals in it (for which it is excellent) you'll probably become eternally grateful for it.

Now I speak as someone who, although I wouldn't be without one, has never taken the time to become a true microwave chef. I am learning but I have never, for example, made cucumber and prawn cheesecake or a stuffed crown roast in my microwave. I was bought up using a conventional oven and I am amazed and in awe of what a microwave can do. My mum doesn't trust them and refuses to make custard in them. My Aunt Jean makes the best custard in the world in a microwave (see page 244).

The basic rules of the microwave are quite simple.

- Never put anything metallic in a microwave. Do not cover dishes you put in the microwave with silver foil.

- You can use heatproof glass or ceramic dishes or dishwasher-safe plastic containers in a microwave.

- If you are cooking something which may splatter, either cover the dish with a microwave lid (a plastic top with holes in it) or cover with a kitchen paper towel.

- Know the power of your machine and follow the recipe instructions accordingly. High is usually Power Level 8 or 9; Medium is Level 6; and Defrost is Level 3.

WHAT TO COOK IN THE MICROWAVE

● Re-heat **ready-made meals**. Simply follow the packet instructions.

● Bags of **frozen vegetables**. Remember to pierce the bag so it doesn't explode.

● **Fish** doesn't shrivel up in the microwave. Arrange the fish so that the thickest parts are to the outside of the dish on the turntable. Cover with pierced cling film. A small fillet of haddock takes about three minutes on High.

● **Jacket potatoes** take hours in a conventional oven but minutes in the microwave. Prick the skin with a fork, then cover the potato with kitchen roll and cook on High for about ten minutes (depending on the size of the potato and whether you are cooking one or more).

● **Aunt Jean's custard** is made from a couple of spoons of custard powder to which you add a little sugar and cold milk, following packet instructions. Then stir in the rest of the pint of cold milk and pop into the microwave for two minutes on High. Take it out and whisk it really well, then cook for another minute. Check, stir and cook for a final minute. As with any liquid in the microwave, make sure you are using a large enough container because, as it heats, the liquid rises.

● Making **scrambled eggs** in the microwave avoids all the tedious cleaning of saucepans. Crack two eggs into a bowl. Beat with a drop of milk. Pop into the microwave on High for about two minutes, stopping to stir it once. Keep an eye on it at the end so you don't over-cook it. (Remember it continues to cook in its own heat when you have removed it.) Season and eat.

● **Hot chocolate** can be very comforting and is dead easy in the microwave. Heat a mug of milk in the microwave on Medium for about two minutes. Stir in three teaspoons of drinking chocolate powder. Enjoy.

- The more items you heat at once, the longer it will take.

- Don't ignore standing times. Food heated in microwaves continues to cook after you have switched it off.

- Stir food when you take it out to get rid of hot spots.

- If you are using the defrost function, make sure you do so at the appropriate level. Do not cook when you mean to defrost.

- Remember food comes out of the microwave scalding hot. The machines are sometimes positioned quite high up and you need to take care when removing items, especially liquids.

- If you cover food with microwaveable cling film, always remember to prick it so that air can escape.

- Always make sure that your food is thoroughly cooked through before eating.

There was this boiled egg, not quite cooked properly. My mum suggested putting it in the microwave. So we did and it exploded. Egg is really annoying to clear up.' MICHAEL, 15

Dear Teenager,
98 HOW TO EAT HEALTHIER TAKE-AWAYS

If you get in the habit of eating take-aways you will be throwing money away and stuffing yourself full of the wrong foods. On the other hand, we all like them once in a while. And if it is only once in a while my view is that you should just enjoy it rather than over-analyse the content and worry about whether it's good for you or not.

However if you are of a mind to choose a healthier option, you can apply common sense and a bit of nutritional understanding and emerge with a full stomach and a few brownie points.

- If you go for a Chinese, say yes to noodle soup and stir fries and plain boiled rice. Say no to fried rice and those tempting prawn crackers and sweet and sour dishes.

- If you go for an Indian, it's yes to the tandoori chicken and the balti dishes and the shish kebabs and more of that boiled rice, and no to onion bhajis and creamy dishes and pilau rice.

- If you go to the chippie, you can eat the fish without the chips or eat the fish but not the batter.

- If you go for a take-away jacket potato, say no to the cheese and sour cream option and yes to the vegetables.

Going for fry-ups at the café isn't going to do you much good. All these things can be done occasionally, but they should constitute a treat, not how you eat day to day. Beans on toast are still going to be better for you nutritionally and financially than slipping out to the greasy spoon.

For other phenomenally easy to prepare foods, remember jacket potatoes, and pasta or rice with almost any sauce on top. Check out the **How to Make Quick Comfort Food** section.

'We eat ready-made meals. I've been known to ring up my friends and say "What can I eat? I've eaten all the ready-made meals in Tesco!" Then I just eat bread and pickles. Luckily in student towns there are usually lots of breakfast bars where you can get all day breakfasts with two eggs and two bacon and coffee and beans for about £3.' TIAN, 20

'Take-aways are a really big issue. They are just such an easy option. You come back late and inevitably you order a Chinese or a pizza and it's really expensive and it tastes horrible.' MATILDA, 20

Dear Teenager,
99 HOW TO MAKE QUICK COMFORT FOOD

There are those nights when you just want a bit of comfort food with no fuss and bother. You want to eat sitting at the kitchen table in your dressing gown or curled up on the sofa in front of the telly. Here are a few ideas. All recipes serve one.

Muffin with bacon and poached eggs
Take:
1 muffin
2 slices of bacon
2 fresh eggs

You can of course make this with bread but the muffin makes it special.

1. Grill your bacon (or microwave it for about 30 seconds a side on high with kitchen paper on top).
2. Poach your eggs like this. Pour about 2 centimetres of water into a frying pan and bring to the boil. Add a splash of vinegar (this prevents the eggs from sticking). Crack an egg into a cup and gently tip into the water. Repeat with the second egg. Cook for about a minute until the egg white is firm and the yolk firm but not solid.
3. Meanwhile split and toast your muffin. Butter it. Place the bacon on top.
4. Using a spatula or fish slice or a spoon if you have nothing better, fish out your eggs and place on top of the bacon.

You can ring the changes by making scrambled eggs instead. To make scrambled eggs, crack two eggs into a bowl and beat with a fork. Add salt and pepper. Melt a walnut-sized dollop of butter in a saucepan. Add your egg mixture and stir continually. Always remove from the heat a little before it is cooked because it continues to cook in the heat of the pan. Alternatively, cook in a microwave but beware of over-cooking it.

Boiled egg and soldiers
Take:
1 egg
a slice of bread
butter
Marmite (optional)

There's nothing wrong with a bit of nursery food sometimes!

1. Place your egg in a small saucepan and cover with cold water.
2. Bring it to the boil, then turn the heat down so the water is gently simmering, not boiling vigorously. Cook for 2½ minutes for soft boiled, or 3 minutes for medium boiled.
3. Lift the egg out of the pan with a dessert spoon and place in an egg cup.
4. Lightly butter a slice of bread (add Marmite if you like) and cut it into fingers.

Some people bash the top of the egg in with a spoon and pick off the shell. I simply slice the top off with a knife. My childhood habit when I've eaten it is then to replace the shell upside down in the cup so that it looks as if you haven't started.

Cheese melt
This is the posh relation to cheese on toast. If you have some not-quite-as-fresh-as-it-should-be baguette, this recipe will transform it into something tasty. It's very nice with soup as well as on its own.

Take:
a piece of baguette
butter
grated cheese
Marmite (optional)
tomatoes (optional)

1. Halve the baguette and lightly toast the outside under a hot grill.
2. Butter the inside. Add Marmite if you love it. Add the grated cheese. Add the tomatoes if you have them.
3. Grill the open baguette for a few minutes until the cheese has melted. Enjoy.

Jacket potato heaven

Jacket potatoes can be just the job and require very little effort. The best baking potatoes are large, floury varieties such as Maris Piper.

1. First of all, scrub the potatoes with a stiff brush to remove any mud, and gouge out the eyes with a small knife.
2. Prick the skin of the potato with a fork before you cook it to stop it exploding.
3. They can be done in minutes in the microwave or you can wrap them in silver foil and leave them in a hot oven (200°C/400°F/gas mark 6) for a few hours. If you like a crispy jacket, leave off the foil.

Topping ideas include: cheese, sweetcorn, ham, tuna, blue cheese, leftover chicken, butter, sour cream, baked beans and coleslaw.

Tuna and Pasta salad

This is also a good way to use up leftover cooked pasta.

Take:
75 g dried pasta (uncooked)
2 chopped tomatoes
half a tin of tuna
half a tin of sweetcorn or some cooked peas
spoonful of mayonnaise

1. Cook your pasta, drain well and leave to cool.
2. Add everything else and mix well. Season with salt and pepper.

Tomato soup deluxe

Take:
1 can tomato soup
1 egg
grated cheese

1. Place an egg in a small saucepan with enough water to cover it. Bring to the boil. Turn the heat down and simmer for 8–10 minutes.
2. Remove the egg from the hot water and cool under a cold tap. Remove shell and halve the egg.
3. Heat the tomato soup in a saucepan. When warmed through, pour into a dish. Add egg and cheese.

'If I could go through it all again, I'd learn to cook before I left home. Budgets are tight and it's the first thing you have to learn, from day one. I'm always ringing up my mum and saying "What do I do now?" and "What temperature should this be at?" I find myself writing lists and recipes and sticking them all over the wall. I've got notes saying BOIL THE RICE FIRST. I've had some disasters.' OLLIE, 18

'The boys were the worst. They just ate pot noodles and bacon sandwiches. Then they'd spend loads of money on fry-ups. Awful. I'm surprised most of them didn't die of malnutrition at the end of the first year. The girls all mucked in and got on with the cooking.' SOPHIE, 22

Comfort food? Hot bananas are very good. Just pop one in foil in the oven for 15 minutes. Sprinkle brown sugar on top. Baked apple is great too. Take the core out of an apple, fill it with brown sugar and pop it in the oven for half an hour.

FIONA SHAW, ACTRESS
(AUNT PETUNIA IN THE *HARRY POTTER* FILMS)

Dear Teenager,
100 HOW TO MAKE A CELEBRATION CAKE

It's always good to have a few tricks up your sleeve and the ability to turn out a cake for a special event is always a winner. Even if it's lop-sided or has sunk or doesn't quite look like the picture book version, people will love the thought and they'll tuck in and love the taste. You can dress up this sponge cake to suit any occasion.

Take:
175 g self-raising flour
1 tsp baking powder
175 g margarine (you need the soft variety for this)
175 g caster sugar
3 eggs, beaten
2 x 18 cm sponge tins
Greaseproof paper

1. Put your oven on (190°C, 375°F or gas mark 5).
2. Grease and line your two tins. You do this by smearing or brushing margarine inside and up the sides of the tins; cut out two circles of greaseproof paper using the base of the tins as a guide; stick the paper in the tins and grease the surface of the paper.
3. Sift the flour and baking powder into a bowl. Add the margarine, sugar and eggs. Beat like hell. If you've got a hand whisk or an electric whisk, use it. If you've got a processor or a mixer, thank your lucky stars. You need to make it smooth and light and lovely.
4. Tip your mixture equally into the two tins. Cook in the preheated oven for 25 minutes. The sponges should be golden and spring back to the touch.
5. Leave to cool for a few minutes, then run a knife around the edges of the tins and tip the cakes out on to a metal rack and allow them to cool completely.

Now you have to think of a filling for your cake. Go wild!

● Sandwich the cakes together with a layer of jam and sprinkle the top with icing sugar through a sieve.

● Sandwich the cakes together with whipped cream and put strawberries or raspberries on top.

● Fill the middle with lemon curd. Heat some lemon juice, add a tablespoon of icing sugar and drizzle over the top of the cake.

● Buy a tub of mascarpone (Italian cream cheese) and an orange. Put the mascarpone into a bowl. Grate the zest of the orange into it. Then squeeze the juice of the orange and strain it into the mascarpone (straining it gets rid of any pips). Beat the mascarpone, adding a couple of teaspoons of icing sugar. Sandwich the cakes with half the mascarpone and spread the rest over the top.

● Don't forget to put some candles on the top as a finishing touch.

'I've made this cake and it's really good.' BEN, 12

AND FINALLY,
when the time comes, how to leave home nicely...

THINKING ABOUT LEAVING HOME IS EXCITING and is, if you're lucky, likely to be a positive experience. It's about growing up and becoming your own person. It's about stretching your wings. Equipped with a bit of training and practice in survival skills, you should be off to a flying start. But spare a thought for your parents.

Although some of them may be relieved to see the back of your disgusting room or your inconsiderate behaviour (surely not!), this is a huge wrench for them. Here's what some of the parents of people quoted in this book have said about the experience.

'I saw an incredible change in Ollie in the first year away. He's far more self-sufficient, confident and more considerate. It's made him grow up. When he comes home now, he appreciates the food and the care he gets at home after having had to fend for himself.

I remember I left home when I got married. I rang my mum up about three weeks later to thank her. It wasn't until I'd left that I realised how much she did, and how much everything cost. You don't realise until you do it for yourself.' OLLIE'S MUM, SUE

'We've noticed a marked increase in indolence! I think he switches off during the holidays. One's always apprehensive when a child leaves. It's as Kahlil Gibran says, "You are the bows from which your children as living arrows are sent forth." You release the string and then all you can do is hold the bow. I have no influence on its flight. Well, I can blow a bit!' WILL'S DAD, MIKE

'I love my mum but I couldn't live with her for long. It's the same with me and Sophie. As soon as she left home we got on much better! In fact she got on with everyone much better as soon as she didn't have to live with them. Now we ring each other all the time and I feel she really appreciates home much more. I really, really miss her but we do get on much better.' SOPHIE'S MUM, SUE

'I didn't do Alexis any favours by doing everything for her. I'm a worrier and after a few experiences of mugging you get more paranoid. But when she left she had no knowledge of banking. She had never written a cheque or used a cash card; she didn't know cheques take five days to clear. Learning to cook also wouldn't have hurt.

Now I speak to her every day. When she's happy I'm happy. When she's unhappy, I get upset for her. She's never really been away from us so it was a bit of an adjustment but now I know she's all right I've stopped worrying about her constantly.' ALEXIS'S MUM, JAN

Dear Teenager,

When you leave home you change the dynamics of the family you are leaving behind. If you are the last child to leave, you are leaving the nest empty. You may feel you have a lot to cope with, but spare a thought for your parents. They have brought you up and cared for you as a toddler and as a spotty, moody adolescent. They have watched you grow and change. I started to worry about my children leaving home when the first one was still in nappies.

Some people feel absolutely ready and eager to leave home, but others feel a little overwhelmed by the prospect. The truth is, it is most likely to be fine and anything you still don't know now, you'll learn as you go along. Leaving home is as exciting rite of passage, so be positive about it.

Remember to call home regularly to let your parents know you are all right. Let them know from time to time how much you appreciate them.

And have a great time!

Dear Parents,

Even as I write this I know I am already dreading my children leaving home. So much of my life is about them. I'd love them to stay at home for ever. But be careful what you wish for. Most of the statistics show that children are remarkably reluctant to leave home these days. More are going to university in their home town and more still are going home to mum in their 20s. Life is increasingly expensive and one way to cope is to live with your parents. You may think as you pack their trunk at 18 that there is no going back, but for many people it turns out that there is. These children are now known as Kippers (kids in parents' back pockets, eroding retirement savings). They are also referred to as boomerangers, thresholders, twixters or parasitic singles. A recent survey suggested that 59 per cent of boys and 39 per cent of girls aged between 20 and 24 live at home with their parents. In a couple of years, your own offspring could be swelling those numbers.

Meanwhile, you need to plan for their departure, whether temporary or permanent. Parents tend to be of the opinion that their kids will never cope without them. After all, they have been waiting on them hand and foot for 18 years. The truth is that most teenagers get by. They may get drunk, eat badly, get into debt and live in a hell-hole but most of them survive the experience. You've done your best for them and tried to teach them a few life skills and now they are on their own. You'll be there for them when they need you, but you can't live their lives for them.

The wrench of parting and of letting go of what you care for most in the world seems encapsulated in the poem on the opposite page. Take a deep breath and let them go.

TO A DAUGHTER LEAVING HOME
Linda Pastan

When I taught you
at eight to ride
a bicycle, loping along
beside you
as you wobbled away
on two round wheels,
my own mouth rounding
in surprise when you pulled
ahead down the curved
path of the park,
I kept waiting
for the thud
of your crash as I
sprinted to catch up,
while you grew
smaller, more breakable
with distance,
pumping, pumping
for your life, screaming
with laughter,
the hair flapping
behind you like a
handkerchief waving
goodbye.

HOW OLD IS OLD ENOUGH?

THE DAY YOU TURN 18, you become a fully fledged adult with adult responsibilities. You are an adult in the eyes of the law. But there is a lot of inconsistency about what you can do when. You may be surprised to see what the law considers you are grown up enough for.

12

● You can now buy a pet without a parent standing in the shop telling you that the cage cleaning is down to you. However there are moves afoot to up the age because animal protection groups think children aren't responsible enough at 12.

● You can also watch 12A movies without an adult, hooray.

13

● You are employable. You can do some part-time work, with restricted hours (two hours a day on school days).

14

● You can now be charged with a criminal offence. Your case will be heard in a juvenile court. (Children are considered capable of crime from the age of ten if it can be proved that they knew what they were doing was wrong.)

● You, not the driver or your mum, are responsible for wearing your own seat belt in the car. If you don't wear it, you can be prosecuted.

● If you live in the country, you can now drive a tractor on farmland.

● You can use an airgun on private premises with the consent of the owner of the premises but you are not allowed to buy it yourself and you are not allowed to buy the pellets for it.

15

● You can get into a certificate 15 film without having to lie about your age.

16

● You can leave school and get a job.

● You can get married if you have parental consent or, in Scotland, without it.

● You can consume alcohol in licensed premises but only with a meal and with an adult. This does not mean a beer with a sandwich or a packet of crisps at the bar, but a proper, substantial meal.

● You can go into some pubs unaccompanied and buy soft drinks. This policy is at the discretion of the licensee.

● You can consent to or refuse medical treatment.

● You can have sex legally.

● You can drive a moped.

● You can win the lottery; you can't buy tickets under 16 years old.

● You can buy cigarettes.

● If you're brave enough, you can fly solo in a glider.

● You can claim benefits and apply for legal aid.

● You now have to pay the full adult fare on the train.

● You can leave home at 16 although you remain in your parents' charge or a ward of court unless you join the armed forces, or marry.

● You can change any part of your name or all of it by deed poll. You simply need a form and a witness and you undertake to use only your new name at all times. You can do it for any reason you like provided that the intention is not fraudulent.

17

● You can drive on the road, in a car, a van or even a tractor.

● You can be a blood donor.

● You can be a street trader.

● You can buy or hire a firearm and apply for a licence. Using imitation firearms in a public place without a good reason is against the law.

● You can apply for a helicopter pilot's licence.

18

● You can be selected for jury service. You are now eligible until you are 70. 450,000 people are called for jury service each year.

● You can get a tattoo.

● You can leave home without parental consent.

● You can vote.

● You can carry an organ donor card and donate organs without parental consent.

● You can buy alcohol.

● You can sell alcohol.

● You can make a will.

● You can buy fireworks.

● You can get married whether your parents like it or not.

● You can apply for a passport without having to get your parents to sign for it.

● You can work in a betting shop and you can place bets.

● You can no longer be fostered or adopted.

● You can buy a property.

● You can see an 18 movie.

21

● You can become an MP or a councillor (although lots of groups are campaigning to make this 18).

● You can drive a heavy goods vehicle.

● You can adopt or foster a child.

RESOURCES

UK

British Dietetic Association
www.bda.uk.com
Information about everything to do with food and nutrition, from making healthy snacks to keeping your heart in shape.

Brook Advisory Centres
www.brook.org.uk
Free, confidential advice on sex, contraception and STIs for teenagers and young people.

Childline
www.childline.org.uk
Free help and advice for children and young people on all types of problems, from bullying to coping with the loss of a loved one.

Citizen's Advice Bureau
www.adviceguide.org.uk
Information and advice on a range of topics including housing, debt and legal issues.

Community Legal Service
www.clsdirect.org.uk
Advice for people seeking legal help, including information on a range of legal topics.

The Electoral Commission
www.aboutmyvote.co.uk
Information on how to register to vote.

Embarrassing Problems
www.embarrassingproblems.com
Advice on awkward health problems and other issues.

The National Community Fire Safety Centre
www.firekills.gov.uk
Advice on preventing fires and what to do in an emergency.

Food Standards Agency
www.eatwell.org.uk
Helpful information on nutrition, health and guidance on under-standing food labels.

Immobilise Property Crime
www.immobilise.com
This website allows you to register your mobile phone, bike and other property so that they can be traced in the event of theft.

Kidscape
www.kidscape.org.uk
Help and information on bullying and abuse for young people.

SunSmart
www.sunsmart.org.uk
Information about staying safe in the sun. This site also directs you to the Met office where you can find the UV rating for the day, so you can measure the degree of risk.

Meningitis Trust
www.meningitis-trust.org
Up-to-date information and advice on meningitis, including infor-mation on vaccines.

Millennium Volunteers
www.millenniumvolunteers.gov.uk
Information for young people who would like to volunteer, includ-ing advice on getting involved in volunteer projects around the UK and abroad.

National Blood Service
www.blood.co.uk
Information on where and how to give blood.

National Union of Students

www.nusonline.co.uk

Help, advice and information for college and university students throughout the UK on a range of issues, from housing to relationships.

NHS Direct

www.nhsdirect.nhs.uk

Information on NHS services throughout the UK, and advice on a range of health concerns and conditions.

Samaritans

www.samaritans.org.uk

Confidential emotional support for people who are experiencing feelings of distress or despair.

St John Ambulance

www.sja.org.uk

First-aid advice, and information on first-aid courses.

Talk to Frank (The National Drugs Helpline)

www.talktofrank.com

Drug advice and help for young people.

The Trident Trust

www.thetridentrust.org.uk

Help for young people seeking work experience placements.

UCAS

www.ucas.ac.uk

Information on applying to study at universities in the UK. The website includes the online UCAS application form.

UK Transplant

www.uktransplant.org.uk

This site has information about organ donation, and has an online form for registering as an organ donor.

Winston's Wish

www.winstonswish.org.uk

Support for grieving children and young people, and their families.

Australia

Arrive Alive
www.arrivealive.com.au
Road safety advice for young drivers.

Beanbag Centres Project
www.beanbag.com.au
A website with the mission to inspire young people. Promotes free internet access.

Here for Life
www.hereforlife.org.au
An organisation and helpline aimed at the prevention of youth suicide.

Kids Helpline
www.kidshelp.com.au
A 24-hour helpline and online counselling service for children and young people.

Lawstuff – The National Children's and Youth Law Centre
www.lawstuff.org.au
Legal information for young people, covering everything from leaving home to criminal courts to tattooing.

Like It Is
www.likeitis.org
A site that offers information about sex and puberty. A good resource for other websites, both local and national.

Money Stuff!
www.moneystuff.net.au
Advice and information for young people on money and living independently.

Reach Out!
www.reachout.com.au
Information for young people, including advice on leaving home.

Schoolies Week
www.goldcoastschoolies.qld.gov.au
Advice on staying safe while partying.

Sexual Health and Hepatitis C Website for Young People
www.istaysafe.com
A sexual health site designed for 13–17 year olds.

The Source
www.thesource.gov.au
Advice for 12–25 year olds about careers, money, their rights, the law, volunteering and more.

Youth Health (Australian Medical Association)
www.ama.com.au/youth
The Australian Medical Association's website for young people.

Youth Substance Abuse Service
www.ysas.org.au
An organisation offering a range of services, including education and support for teens experiencing problems with alcohol and drugs.

New Zealand

Community Alcohol and Drug Service (CADS)
www.cads.org.nz
Help and advice for people with addiction problems. This site also has a good section about safer partying, and provides information on drink spiking and drugs.

Everybody
www.everybody.co.nz
A medical directory of ailments, plus advice.

StudentHUB
www.studenthub.co.nz
A site for students, with advice on accommodation, studying and student issues. Has an extensive contacts list.

Studyit

www.studyit.org.nz

Advice and study tips for National Certificate of Educational Achievement (NCEA) students.

Youthline

www.youthline.co.nz

A site which offers a confidential youth helpline. You can phone, or you can email: *talk@youthline.co.nz*.

The Word

www.theword.org.nz

A site for young people offering information on sex, relationships and abuse.

South Africa

Learning Channel

www.learn.co.za

Study tips and help for high school students.

Love Life

www.lovelife.org.za

A site for parents and teenagers about sex and relationships, including advice on HIV and other STIs. Promotes a healthy lifestyle.

South African Youth Information Service

www.yis.co.za

An organisation providing information on a range of issues, from money to staying healthy.

TeenGrowth

www.teengrowth.com

Information about bodies, health, school, friends and family.

Umsobomvu Youth Fund

www.uyf.org.za

An organisation providing information and opportunities for education and employment for young South Africans.

INDEX

OTHER RODALE BOOKS
AVAILABLE FROM PAN MACMILLAN

1-4050-3337-1 978-1-4050-3337-4	The Acne Cure	*Terry J Dubrow and* *Brenda D Adderly*	£10.99
1-4050-0675-7 978-1-4050-0675-0	The Secret Life of the Dyslexic Child	*Robert Frank and* *Kathryn E Livingston*	£10.99
1-4050-7732-8 978-1-4050-7732-3	How to Help Your Overweight Child	*Karen Sullivan*	£12.99
1-4050-4182-X 978-1-4050-4182-9	The Doctor's Book of Home Remedies	*Dr Stephen Amiel*	£20.00
1-4050-6729-2 978-1-4050-6729-4	When Difficult Relatives Happen to Good People	*Dr Leonard Felder*	£10.99
1-4050-8812-5 978-1-4050-8812-1	Pregnancy Questions & Answers	*The Editors of* *BabyCentre.co.uk*	£14.99

All Rodale/Pan Macmillan titles can be ordered from the website,
www.panmacmillan.com, or from your local bookshop and are also available
by post from:

Bookpost, PO Box 29, Douglas, Isle of Man IM99 1BQ
Tel: 01624 677237; fax: 01624 670923; e-mail: *bookshop@enterprise.net*; or
visit: *www.bookpost.co.uk.* Credit cards accepted. Free postage and packing in
the United Kingdom

Prices shown above were correct at time of going to press.
Pan Macmillan reserve the right to show new retail prices on covers which may
differ from those previously advertised in the text or elsewhere.

For information about buying *Rodale* titles in **Australia,** contact Pan Macmillan
Australia. Tel: 1300 135 113; fax: 1300 135 103;
e-mail: *customer.service@macmillan.com.au*; or visit:
www.panmacmillan.com.au

For information about buying *Rodale* titles in **New Zealand,** contact Macmillan
Publishers New Zealand Limited. Tel: (09) 414 0356; fax: (09) 414 0352;
e-mail: *lyn@macmillan.co.nz*; or visit: *www.macmillan.co.nz*

For information about buying *Rodale* titles in **South Africa,** contact Pan
Macmillan South Africa. Tel: (011) 325 5220; fax: (011) 325 5225;
e-mail: *marketing@panmacmillan.co.za*